051

He   ~ Garage

Running
A to Z

1

27
26
—
53
52
—
106
2650
—
275.6
3
—
8268

27
52
—
54
1350
—
1404
3
—
4202

| 1401 |
| 5 |
| 7,005 | } 5,000

Running _A to Z_

An Encyclopedia for the Thoughtful Runner

by

Joe Henderson

The Stephen Greene Press
Lexington, Massachusetts

To George Sheehan, a second father

First Edition

Text copyright © 1983 by Joe Henderson

This book is manufactured in the United States of America. It is designed by Irving Perkins Associates and published by The Stephen Greene Press, Lexington, Massachusetts. Distributed by Viking Penguin Inc.

Library of Congress Cataloging in Publication Data

Henderson, Joe 1943–
Running A to Z.

Includes index.
1. Running. I. Title.
GV1061.H394   1983   796.4'26   82–25109
ISBN 0–8289–0504–5 (pbk.)

PUBLISHED MARCH 1983
Reprinted 1983 (twice), 1984, 1985

Contents

Personal Notes

THIS BOOK ASSUMES several things about you who read it. Some of these notions may or may not fit. But a writer has to feel he knows his readers—what they want and what he should give them—or the book lacks focus.

I have run and written about running for a long time, and I have raced everything from sprints to ultramarathons, never having great competitive success.

You probably are already a runner, so I don't need to spend any time converting you. You want to be a better runner—perhaps a faster one, certainly a healthier and happier one.

You know many of the ideas and people of running. You probably have read other running books (there are plenty to choose from), but you've chosen this one because its author gives you a somewhat different slant on things (thank you for paying me this compliment).

You know that most of the ideas here are not original. I draw them from the pool of common running knowledge and sometimes fail to give proper credit to the original source. However, I don't plead plagiarism. A writer plagiarizes when he steals material from one person. When he borrows from many, as I do here, he calls his work "research."

You know that although I avoid using the word "I" after

these notes end, every one of the "rules of the road" has sifted through my biases. You know, too, that each of them has been tested by my own experience, has stood up to the wear and tear of time, and been found worthy of publication here.

You know that I don't expect you to take every printed word as gospel. Your experience can never precisely match mine, so you can take only what fits into your own grand research project.

You know that you want to keep running for life. Fitness is important to you, and so is racing. You would keep running even if science proved that the physical risks of the activity outweighed the benefits. You would keep running even if your racing times slipped and you lost all chances to race.

You know that you enjoy the sport as much for the little pleasures it gives you daily as for the big victories over ill health and other runners that it might or might not give you far down the road.

You know that you've built your own running on firm ground and that you are part of a community of runners which forms a solid foundation for the sport.

I think of that running community as historian Will Durant thought of the world at large. He called it "a stream with banks." Most writers, he said, watch only the rush and swirl of the water, "which is sometimes filled with blood from people killing, stealing, shouting." Durant paid most of his attention to the activity on the river banks—"where unnoticed people build homes, make love, raise children, sing songs, write poetry . . ."

The flow of major running events isn't unimportant. I often write about and you often read of the performance and business and political news made by a few runners. But most of this news has little to do with you and your everyday running. Most of you watch the flood race past as you quietly move through your life on the banks.

I write here of you and for you, the 99 percent of runners whose running goes unnoticed 99 percent of the time.

Joe Henderson
Eugene, Oregon
October, 1982

"I travel not to go anywhere, but to go."

—ROBERT LOUIS STEVENSON

"For every runner who tours the world running marathons, there are thousands who run to hear the leaves and listen to the rain, and look to the day when it is suddenly as easy as a bird in flight. For them, sport is not a test but a therapy, not a trial but a reward, not a question but an answer."

—GEORGE SHEEHAN

Running
A to Z

A

Approaches and Attitudes

PACING FOR A LIFETIME

ANNE BROWNE SAT at the breakfast table. She wore running shoes and shorts, an oversized T-shirt, and a contented smile.

"If only all my runs could be as nice as this one was," she said. "I still am trying to get to the level where running is as fun as you say it's supposed to be. Most days, I have to force myself out the door. About half the time, the lazy side of me wins this battle."

The runner across the table admitted that he, too, was still trying to climb to the level where running was fun every day. He said, "I've tried and failed for more than 20 years to make it that way. I've run some 7500 mornings, and on at least half of them I've argued with the lazier side of me that wants to stay in bed."

"I've kept running," he added after sipping his tea, "be-

1

cause I know the hardest step is always the first one out the door. And I keep going because I never know until after I start if this run is going to be a perfect one. When everything is flowing just right, there's no feeling like it. I'd wade through a lot of bad runs to find one of those."

Running never has been, never will be, and maybe never even *should* be fun every step of the way. Any writer who claims otherwise leads readers to expect something that running can't deliver. On the other hand, anyone who writes that running is always painful and boring misleads readers even more. He makes them think running is bitter medicine that people hate but tolerate because it's good for them.

The truth sits between these extreme views. Running doesn't hurt all the time, only sometimes. It isn't fun all the time, only sometimes. We try to reduce the pain and increase the joy to the point where the net effect is positive. If it is, we'll keep running.

In 1969, Kenny Moore answered a questionnaire mailed to many of the country's leading runners. He was an Olympic marathoner then and not yet a *Sports Illustrated* writer, but his thorough and thoughtful answers to the questions portended the writer he would be.

When asked how and why he had started running, Moore wrote, "The reasons people start running are rather standard and mundane. The more significant question would be what *keeps* them running."

Why do some runners continue and thrive, while many with equal starting talent and enthusiasm drop out? A few years ago, a survey showed that nine in ten of the runners active on one New Year's Day wouldn't be running by the next January 1st. The survival rate has improved since then, thanks to better training advice and support for new runners. But running still loses as many as half of its recruits from year to year.

The two main reasons why runners become former runners are disability and discouragement. The causes of this physical and emotional paralysis most often are goals set too high and runs done too fast. Consider the case of Jeff King:

The first of these problems almost made King an ex-runner before he'd really gotten started. "I expected to win or at least place well in my first race," he recalls. "Never mind that I hadn't raced before, had trained only two weeks, and was years younger and inches smaller than anyone else running. My coach had told me I could do anything if I tried hard enough."

Jeff tried. He ran his best time for a quarter-mile. Unfortunately, this was a *mile* race. Everyone passed him on the second lap before he dropped out—out of the race and out of running, for all he cared. His brother pulled him through this first crisis.

"That was a stupid thing to do," the older brother said as Jeff stood beside the track, looking down at his barely used spiked shoes as the lecture continued. "Well, it's done. Now quit feeling sorry for yourself. You thought you were a world-beater, and now you know you're not. You can't keep up with guys who've been running longer than you have. Big deal!"

Jeff, in 1958, was listening to advice that would become a theme of the 1970s and 1980s running boom: "You can't think you have to beat everyone. That will drive you crazy. You'll always be disappointed, because no matter how good you get, there'll always be someone better. Compete only with yourself. Try for your own best times. That way, no one can beat you but yourself."

Years later, Jeff beat himself into a second crisis. Times meant everything to him. He not only kept records for races and tried to break them every week, he also timed his training runs and tried to go faster every day.

"This excited me at first," he says, "when I could knock off clumps of time without really trying. Then progress slowed. I worked harder and harder for less and less improvement. Finally I raced myself daily and didn't improve at all.

I could live with that, but not with the chronic lower-leg pain and fatigue that went with the speeding.

"I backed off to a gentler pace just to save my legs and found that the change gave me a whole new view of running that I'd never seen while staring at the numbers on a watch."

King's worst mistakes taught him about setting realistic goals and then about running at a sensible pace. These lessons point to a "survival plan" that starts this way:

- *Goals*—Keep them personal and general. Don't compare yourself with anyone's standards except your own. Make it your main goal simply to keep running. Don't let your specific sub-goals conflict with that future.
- *Paces*—Pace your entire running career as if it were a long race. You wouldn't race yourself dry in the first mile of a marathon, leaving nothing for the next 25 miles. So don't run today like there is no tomorrow. Hold something in reserve for later.

NOT-SO-LONG, NOT-SO-SLOW DISTANCE

LSD MEANS LONG, Slow Distance to a runner. When that method took its name in the 1960s, "long" meant anything longer than the track races, "slow" meant anything slower than track-racing pace, and "distance" meant anything more than the 25 miles a week needed as training for track.

Time has devalued distance and pace. The daily five-to-six-mile runs at a comfortable seven-to-eight-minute pace, totaling 40-to-50-mile weeks now seem short, rather fast, and inadequate in total distance. Time has left some of us so far behind that we now prefer the term "gentle running" to LSD.

However, the original words still work for defining a survival technique: long, but not too long; slow enough to go long enough, and not the most distance you can do but the least you need.

How Long? Janet Lee had done her mile or two a day, six days a week, for a few years. She liked the way these runs made her feel afterward but, frankly, didn't care much for the running itself. She ran with about as much enthusiasm as she put into washing the kitchen floor.

Then Janet started working full time. She could only run a few days a week, so she doubled the amount, going three or four miles at a time. Her outlook on running changed dramatically, from tolerating it for the results to liking the runs themselves.

"The extra distance made the difference," she says. "I wasn't going far enough before to know that running could feel good."

This effect seems to break the laws of mathematics, physiology, and common sense. If one mile feels bad, two should hurt twice as much. But that doesn't happen when we run. We need a few miles for warm-up before the real running can begin. This first half-hour can be boring and painful, even for longtime runners. We put up with this period to get to the good part in the second half-hour.

Any number of scientists can prove that most of the physical benefits of a run come in that first period. Dr. Kenneth Cooper, author of *Aerobics*, says 12 minutes is the optimum running time. After that, the returns diminish. The first 30 minutes certainly make us fit, but the second 30 make running worth doing and make us want to keep coming back for more.

Tip One, then, is: *Always go at least 30 minutes but rarely more than an hour.*

How Slow? Dr. George Sheehan, the sport's leading medical commentator, says the fitness formula has three elements: "The running should be of a specific intensity, for a specific length of time, done a specific number of times a week. The aim is to do 30 minutes four times a week at a pace somewhere between easy and hard."

The hardest of these requirements to satisfy, Sheehan says, is pace: "If the pace is too slow, it does very little good. On the other hand, a too-fast pace is self-defeating."

He tells of a woman friend with the second, and far more common, pacing problem.

"I can't run more than a half-mile," she complained. "No matter what I do, I'm finished at that point."

The doctor went running with her, and she covered several times her normal distance, talking all the way.

"I've never run that slow!" she exclaimed.

"That was the answer, of course," Dr. Sheehan says. The pace had been slow enough to allow normal conversation, slow enough to allow a half-hour of comfortable effort.

"Comfortable" is the key word. George Sheehan tells runners to set their inner dials just below the discomfort zone, then to stay there, easing off the pace whenever it starts to hurt.

Tip Two: *Run at a comfortable, gentle pace—not too fast or too slow*.

How Much Distance? You never know where you'll meet a marathoner these days. As a stewardess was working the cabin on a flight out of San Diego, she noticed that a passenger was reading a running magazine.

"Oh, do you run, too?" she asked.

She said she'd run for a few months and was now getting ready for the Heart of San Diego Marathon.

"I went 14 miles today," she matter-of-factly told the passenger.

"Great. Is that your long run of the week?" he said, thinking he was praising her.

"Oh, no. Tomorrow I'm running 20 miles. How much do you run?"

"Uh . . . um . . . ," he stuttered. "Enough." He couldn't bring himself to tell her he had never run 14 and 20 miles two days in a row, even though he was a veteran of two dozen marathons. And she hadn't asked for advice, so he didn't tell her she was making two common mistakes.

The first was thinking anyone needs that kind of mileage for anything but serious marathon racing. She only wanted to finish, and she could have done that on half the running she was doing.

Her second mistake was thinking that training is all work and no recovery. Not even serious racers do long runs back to back as she did. They give themselves at least one and usually several easy days after every hard one so they won't run themselves down. The mileage doesn't add up as quickly this way, but the training is both more effective and more pleasant.

Tip Three: *Stay fresh and eager by mixing hard and easy, long and short races and runs.*

This is *not* a chapter about how to race, but about how to keep running. Of course, if racing contributes to that end, please race. Just heed one warning and accept one assurance.

The warning: Racing does nothing for physical fitness and, in fact, usually tears you down temporarily. The assurance: Everyone who races can feel like a winner, and that feeling blots out the exhaustion. A final story illustrates both points.

Life had always been easy for this Chicago woman, the wife of a prominent business executive. She could afford to ride any distance she wanted in a chauffeured Rolls Royce. But she chose to run 26 miles, 385 yards. She finished slowly, painfully, two hours behind the leaders.

Her husband later said that she couldn't get out of bed for

a day and a half. "She was so stiff, she could hardly move. I might have been tempted to call a doctor or move her to a hospital—except all the time she kept moaning what a *fantastic* experience it was, and how she wanted to do it again next year."

The new marathoner's husband, who had recently bought her an expensive piece of jewelry, told the race director, "You gave her a piece of paper for finishing your race that probably cost 10 cents. Yet if she had to choose between the emerald and the paper, I know what the choice would be."

This is all you need to know about running technique. Much more can and will be said, but beyond these words, the rest is commentary:

> *You need to use only two speeds, running and racing. The first is easy, the second hard. The first builds up; the second tears down.*
>
> *The trick to successful, enjoyable, lasting running and racing is to repair more than you tear. Make the bulk of efforts "runs."*
>
> *Run on the borderline between comfort and discomfort; race on the line between discomfort and destruction. Run daily, doing nothing on any running day that you would not or could not do every day. Race no more than once a week, and do no race-like "training" on days meant for recovery and rebuilding.*

B

Basic Survival Plan

ONE BIG DAY IN 10

ONE RUNNER'S LAZINESS is another's cunning. Others may call you lazy; you choose to think of yourself as smart. You don't believe in wasting effort, and much of what goes into runners' diaries as "good, hard work" is as wasted as a second cup of coffee they try to pour into a container with room for just one.

One Saturday, you raced. You pushed yourself hard, because a race isn't real unless you run it all-out. That day, you strung together six sub-six-minute miles on a rough cross-country course. You rarely run more than six miles or faster than an *eight*-minute pace when not racing. One reason you can get this much from this little is the cunning that comes with experience. Another reason is that you don't waste much effort between races.

The Sunday after this race, you tiptoe through the previous day's destruction. You'd beaten yourself up and now

9

try not to land any new blows. This day is meant for recovery, as are the next several days.

A friend who hadn't raced meets you on the road. He has to cut back his pace by a minute a mile to match yours.

He needles you: "How can you race so fast one day and run so slowly the next?"

You answer in kind: "How come I can never stay with you on runs like this, and you can never stay with me when it comes time to go all-out?"

This morning at a Fun Run, you see another friend.

"I missed you at the race yesterday," you say.

"I took a long one," he tells you. "I'm getting ready for a marathon."

You say good for him to show enough restraint to pass up a race in favor of long training. What you don't ask, though, is why he isn't showing the same restraint the next day. He is running a hard 10 kilometers instead of letting the effects of the long run pass.

You passed up the Fun Run, except to amble down to the start from home to say hi to friends. That done, you amble the couple of miles back home. On the way, you see three more runners you know. All had raced the day before.

One has run for less than a year, so she can be excused for her eagerness. She wants it all—now. She wants to break 40 minutes for 10 K *and* to become an ultramarathoner. So after running close to her first goal in Saturday's race, she is training for the second one with a 25-mile run today.

The other two runners illustrate what often happens after someone races. He has either done better than expected, or worse.

In the first case, the usual reaction is, "Gee, if I did that well on that much training, think how much better I could do with more."

After a failure, the thinking goes, "The reason I did so poorly is that I haven't trained enough. I'll have to start doing more."

Both try to make their changes immediately. The next runner you meet had raced very well the day before—two minutes faster than normal. That inspired him to run 17 miles early Sunday morning. The other runner had raced poorly—a minute slower than normal. He punishes himself now by pushing through 10 miles.

Your experience—you've made all of these mistakes yourself—tells you that everyone you see this Sunday morning is doing something wasteful. Your kind of laziness is the only proper response after a hard day's work.

Bill Bowerman stands tallest among running theorists who say that more runners overwork than underwork. Among serious runners (those of us who race and are in this game for life), probably nine in ten run too much.

We're not simply talking about hard work. It is our right, even our duty, as runners to go too far or too fast once in a while. The nature of racing is carrying running to the extremes of effort.

No, the big problem we have isn't working too hard itself. It is working too hard, *too often*, not taking enough time to recover and rebuild from our excesses.

An axiom of the sport states that work and recovery are equal parts of the running puzzle. But they aren't equal. The recovery is much more important than the work—perhaps ten times more important. That's because we tear down quickly but rebuild slowly. It takes as many easy days to repair the damage of a single hard run.

This leads to a better formula for combining work and recovery: a "Big One" each week or two at the limits of distance or speed; all other runs are to recover-rebuild from this Big One.

Jeff Galloway—Olympian, running-shop entrepreneur, advisor to hundreds of novice runners, southern gentleman—inspired the formula.

"The only run that really counts is the hard one," Jeff

drawls. "Make sure that one is good and hard, and you don't have to worry about what you do the rest of the time."

He tells of the many runners he has helped toward marathons. The biggest mistakes they had made earlier were (1) running too far in midweek, and (2) not running far enough on weekends.

Jeff gets them to quit adding up weekly mileage. He says it isn't important. All that really matters is pushing up toward the full marathon distance on the long one, then recovering the rest of the time with short runs. He doesn't even give a long one every week at first, only every second week. He says most beginners need that long to recoup their losses. He starts everyone at one mile above their current longest distance and steps up by just a mile every other week. In between, he calls for no runs longer than eight miles, preferably something in the three-to-five range.

The Galloway Formula applies to all types of Big Ones, fast as well as long: only one run every week or two treated as big/hard/special; everything else small/easy/casual.

Garry Bjorklund had flown to Hawaii straight from a Minnesota winter and was taking a 200-mile training week. When asked what he'd be doing if he were at home, he said flatly, "Two hundred." He made it clear that he would have worn more clothes, wouldn't have enjoyed himself as much, but would have reached his quota even if he had stayed in Minneapolis. The Hawaiian trip was just a lucky break.

Bjorklund ran his 200 miles, disintegrating steadily as the week progressed. On the first day, he was a normal, rational, energetic human being. By week's end, he could barely walk or talk straight. He finished his 200-mile binge with a marathon and another six miles later that day.

Garry didn't do this every week. He couldn't have stood it. He explained that he ran by three-week cycles. This obviously was his big-mileage week. He would follow it with an easy week when he might do as little as five miles a day. Then he would complete the cycle with a week emphasizing speed.

He kept repeating those cycles through the winter of 1980. He had been pointing toward the U.S. Olympic Trial Marathon in May. But when the boycott of the Russian games took away the lure of that race, he switched his attention to the Grandma's Marathon near his home. He ran it in 2:10:19—identical to the winning time at the "Trial."

Few of us have designs on such world-class marathoning or would ever consider running a 200-mile week. Yet we might heed the prediction of Dr. Ernst van Aaken. The German physician-coach said 30 years ago that the training pattern of the future would be no different for the champion athlete than the person running for fitness. The champ would run more, certainly, because he must. He would run faster, because he was able. But his general plan would look much like everyone else's.

The future is here. We all run like the big guys, only not as long or as fast. We do our everyday running about a minute per mile slower than race pace, just as they do. We, like they, do about 90 percent of our running gently and 10 percent hard. The only differences are the amounts and paces involved.

We can and should follow a pattern similar to Garry Bjorklund's and Jeff Galloway's:

> • A long *weekend* (rather than a full week, a la Bjorklund)—at the long end of our racing range.
> • A fast weekend—at the short end of that range.
> • A weekend of neither distance nor speed— coasting through it with normal running.

This averages out to a Big One every 10 days. That is all most of us need and all that we can tolerate without running the risk of big troubles.

PLAYING THE PERCENTAGES

JOHN KRAMER KNOWS and obeys and follows the 10-percent speed limit now, but he was a long time learning it. Back in college, he shot up to doing hard work more than half of the time. He paid for it most dramatically with an achilles tendon injury that still bothers him. This constant hammering hurt him in other subtle ways. Looking back, John is sure that it cost him the 4:10 to 4:12 mile that he knows he had in him then.

"Look at the evidence," he says. "I went 4:18 in the second big meet of the outdoor season my junior year. Before the third, I trained on three interval half-miles at 2:05, 2:03, and 2:01 with just a lap of recovery between. If this didn't show 4:12 mile ability, I don't know what does. A few days later, I breezed through a three-quarter-mile trial in 3:08. I could have gone another lap at the same pace."

The day after that, a calf muscle tore. John sat in the stands that weekend, watching teammates—4:18 milers like himself—improve to the 4:12 range.

Persistent calf and then achilles problems finally drove him out of speed training altogether. But he still took a long time after that to learn how little speed of any kind he could mix into his formula.

"I stopped training for speed in 1966," Kramer says. "But I kept *racing* for it. For the five of the next six years, I raced above my speed limit, because I still didn't know exactly what it was.

"The exception was 1968, when I stumbled onto the right combination of hard and easy running. This was probably my healthiest and most productive racing year ever. I ran at or near PRs (personal records) from the mile through 30 kilometers and never had a hint of an injury or illness. In no month did I ever exceed one fast mile in 10."

Kramer would never race that well again. In 1969, he

came down with persistent bronchitis; in 1970, a calf-muscle tear; in 1971, achilles tendinitis; in 1972, bursitis of the heel. None of this was bad luck. There is very little bad luck in running—every problem John had fell into a pattern. Looking back with 20-20 hindsight, he now sees that every injury and illness was predictable and preventable. He had made his own "luck."

His diary shows:

> **October 1969**   18-percent racing the month that bronchitis began.
> **October 1970**   Raced 16 percent of the time in the month that the calf muscle tore.
> **October 1971**   The month of the achilles breakdown featured 22-percent racing.
> **May 1972**   A 23-percent racing binge set off the bursitis.

"I wouldn't run without a limp again for more than a year," Kramer says. "That year included surgery to remove an offending bone growth on the right heel and a month off my feet completely. Only then did I take exact stock of how high a toll this racing extracted."

He backed up and looked at the old figures. They told him that if the percentage of racing was too low—say, two percent or less—he didn't do well; he felt stiff, awkward and sluggish from not being used to the pace. If the amount landed between five and ten percent, he felt his best and raced his best; he was doing enough racing but not too much. If he went over ten percent . . . well, you've heard those results.

Kramer still keeps percentages after the fact, at the end of each month. But he needed a way to look ahead, too, to set a danger zone after racing, a time when any more hard work would put him at risk.

New Zealander Jack Foster offered a simple formula: one week or one day per racing mile, whichever is longer. After a race of 10 kilometers or less, for instance, allow an easy week to recover; after a half-marathon, two weeks; after a full marathon, almost a full month.

C

Clothes and Shoes

Between You and the Road

A FREQUENT SPEAKER on the running-clinic circuit often introduces himself at his talks by saying, "People expect to see someone older and taller." They think anyone with his credentials as a running authority must have gray hair and be larger than life.

"Before I started running," the speaker says, "I was six-feet-two. You all know that running takes off weight. But a side effect that no one talks about is that it also takes off height by pounding you down."

He is joking. He grows slightly more serious when he talks about age: "My face may not look 80 years old, but my feet feel that way. A podiatrist has estimated that for every year of running, the feet age by four years. I have the feet to prove the wisdom of that statement."

Feet that have spent years on the road need coddling if they are to keep giving reliable service into truly old age. You

might be tempted to conclude from this evidence of acceler-
ated aging that babying the feet means putting more and
more cushioning between them and the unyielding surfaces.
That has been the fashion in running shoemaking, at least
among U.S. companies, for a decade.

One publication took a foreign company to task for trying
to reverse that trend. In an article titled "Let Them Eat Concrete," *Running Commentary* quoted Horst Widman of
Adidas: "World-class runners don't like shoes with a lot of
shock absorption. We are fighting our (U.S.) distributors
who are constantly imploring us to make butter-soft shoes.
We don't want this. It's against our philosophy. One day,
people in the United States will understand this."

The *Commentary's* response: "Those runners who actually pay for shoes—instead of being paid to wear them—
aren't for the most part 140-pounders who seem to glide
along a foot above the ground. Most buyers need more rub-
ber between themselves and the road."

This statement brought quick rebuttals. Longtime runner
Desmond O'Neill argued with the newsletter's praise of soft
shoes.

"I don't agree at all," wrote O'Neill. "I have felt for a long
time that very well-cushioned shoes have not been particularly desirable. And I had far fewer problems of my own with
the flat, comparatively uncushioned shoes of yesteryear than
I do with some of the flared, flanged, and fully cushioned
models of today."

A similar argument came from Jack Foster. No one his
age has ever run a faster marathon, and few have younger
feet in their 50th year.

Jack wrote, "I was introduced to serious running over New
Zealand farmlands, where the underfoot conditions were soft
and yielding, and one developed good strength and flexibility. I ran in light tennis shoes. There were no training flats
in those days. We ran in those flimsy, light shoes and developed a 'feel' for the ground. We learned to land properly or

got sore legs. We couldn't rely on the shoes to absorb any shock, so we got into a light-footed gait which moved us over hill and dale very efficiently. I'm certain this helped me stay injury-free."

Foster added, "I continue to run daily in shoes which most people consider too light even for racing."

The message from these two runners seems to be: Wear the least padding you can stand. A man who helped revolutionize the product doesn't fully agree or necessarily disagree. He says it depends on whose feet the shoes go on.

Jeff Johnson was for years in charge of research and development for Nike, where he designed its top-of-the-line models. Much earlier, he conducted the first published running-shoe survey. However, he now criticizes the rationale behind such ratings.

"In recent years," he says, "magazine shoe surveys annually attempted to rank shoes against criteria which the editors deemed worthwhile. The premise of every such survey was that certain characteristics of a shoe were good, that more was better—and that it was better for everyone. The magazines, for example, concluded that if cushioning was a good thing, more of it was better and that all runners should place equal value on well-cushioned shoes.

"What all surveys ignored, of course, is that the needs of different runners vary widely. While well-cushioned shoes are generally lauded by the population with rigid feet, they create problems for flexible feet which generally need stability and motion control."

Johnson has guided Nike toward "designing and marketing specific shoes for the different needs of the running population. Happily, other shoe manufacturers have begun to follow suit and to support their development work with responsible research. Now even the magazines have begun to stress information over 'rankings.'"

Johnson says, "It is now contingent on the shoe manufacturers to communicate their research results and product information clearly. It is the responsibility of serious runners to learn their particular needs. Neither is an easy task, for responding to different runners' needs has necessarily led to a proliferation of products. But the rewards of finding the shoe that ranks number one in your own personal survey is well worth all of our efforts."

When selecting shoes, you have only two loyalties: to your left foot and your right. Your feet tell you what they want. Theirs is the only shoe survey that counts.

WHAT TO WEAR WHEN

WEATHER TELLS YOU what to wear. Add or subtract layers of clothes, depending on how hot or cold the day is.

This advice would be too obvious to mention, if runners would only remember the "20-Degree Rule." They dress comfortably for standing still, then grow uncomfortably—even intolerably—hot after the first mile of running.

The rule states that the temperature automatically climbs by 20 degrees during a run. A nice 70-degree day suddenly feels like a steamy 90; a chilling 30 becomes a pleasant 50.

Dress with this rule in mind. The right clothes for running are the ones that seem too skimpy while you stand still. This means you have to build this 20-degree factor into a rating of clothing needs.

"Hot" is a thermometer reading of 90 degrees or higher while sitting or moving slowly. But that borderline drops to about 70 on the run.

"Warm" is weather in the 70s and 80s during resting hours, but in the 50s and 60s while running.

You feel "cool" when you lounge about in temperatures between the low 50s and the high 60s, and when running at slightly above the freezing mark.

When you're not working hard, anything below 50 may seem "cold." But that cold-weather line may drop well below 30 when you run.

Start dressing each day with a foundation of socks, shoes and shorts. The wardrobe builds from there:

> • *Hot.* Add only the lightest top that modesty will allow.
> • *Warm.* Add a T-shirt.
> • *Cool.* Add long pants, and a long-sleeved shirt or light jacket.
> • *Cold.* Add a layer of protection for the hands and ears, and perhaps another layer on the legs and face for extreme cold.

The rainsuits now popular serve both to keep out cold without adding bulk or restricting movement and to repel water. On rainy days, add a cap with a bill to keep your vision clear.

This is the basic running uniform, designed for function rather than fashion.

INS AND OUTS

THE PARADE PASSES BY. Fashions come ond go. The styles of the time when this book was written may not be the same as those when it is read, so be alert for changes. The parade looks this way in 1983:

> • *In* are burgundy, beige, and silver shoes. *Out* is the old standby, blue. *Way out*—white leather.
> • White half-socks have come *in* style. No socks and knee-high socks are equally *out*. Colored stretch socks—*way out.*

• *In* for cool-weather training are long nylon pants. *Out*—baggy gray sweats. *Way out*—sweats with shorts on the outside.

• Old race T-shirts are *in* for training wear. Race singlets are *out* except when racing. Unmarked undershirts are *way out*.

• *In* are baseball-style caps. *Out* are headbands. *Way out*—headphones.

• The *in* runner races in European-cut shorts, the kind that would have been outlawed as obscene a few years ago. The *out* racer wears cotton gym shorts. *Way out*—cutoff Levis.

• The *in* racer wears a mesh singlet. *Out* are male racers without a shirt. Wearing a T-shirt from the race being run is *way out*.

• Anyone sporting a black digital watch belongs to the *in*-crowd. Anyone carrying a stopwatch while running is *out*. Wearing no watch and claiming not to care about time is *way out*.

• It is *in* to fold, tear, or otherwise mutilate racing numbers to make them smaller . . . *out* to race with no number as an "outlaw" . . . *way out* to pin the number on your back.

• Count yourself as *in* if you wear running shoes when not running . . . *out* if you wear full running uniforms to the grocery store . . . *way out* if you wear the same clothes all day after running in them.

The styles extend beyond what you wear. To be truly *in*, you must call yourself a "serious runner." You must say you are "training to improve at the shorter distances." You must never admit to doing anything but high-quality training. You must say, "I began running a long time ago—before it was *in*."

D

Diet and Drinks

No-Nonsense Eating

No subject in running needs less dogma and more humor than this one. Normally sensible and funny people turn into zealots when the talk turns to food and drink. We want to believe in magic—either that magical things will happen if we put something new into ourselves or if we take something old out.

Dr. George Sheehan has been both running and eating for a long time. He hasn't noticed any magic being worked with a knife, fork, or spoon. The only secrets are spelled M-I-L-E-S and P-A-C-E, and no supermarket carries those.

Good storyteller that he is, Dr. Sheehan leads into this subject with an anecdote: "When noted running researcher Dr. David Costill did a physiological profile on marathoner Bill Rodgers, he learned something about Rodgers' eating habits." He didn't learn it from any complex tests but from observations that hardly were scientific.

"Costill was eating lunch in the laboratory when Rodgers arrived, so Dave invited him to sit down for some preliminary discussion," says Sheehan.

Rodgers, normally the best of talkers, seemed preoccupied. Instead of looking at Costill, he stared at Dave's dessert. Realizing that his research would go nowhere as long as they had this barrier between them, Costill finally said, "Would you like this piece of pie, Bill?"

It was eaten almost before the doctor had finished his question.

Bill Rodgers' appetite and food preferences are almost as legendary as his running ability. George Sheehan says, "Like many high-mileage runners, Rodgers is a junk-food junkie. These elite runners will eat almost anything, but they lean toward cake and pie, candy and pastry, soft drinks and beer."

Sheehan quotes a study of South African marathoners who did only half as much running as Rodgers. They averaged 56 miles a week—and 76 teaspoons of sugar a week.

"This sugar represented only 40 percent of their carbohydrate intake. Candy, pastries, cake, bisquits, and soft drinks were major sources of this foodstuff."

Sheehan, the cardiologist, sees nothing scandalous in taking so much of the substance that some think of as one step removed from rat poison.

"Apparently, this is the diet that runners' instincts tell them is best. As their mileage increases, so does their need for quick-energy 'junk food.'

"Running affects the 'appestat,'" Sheehan continues. "This is the instinct which tells us what, when, and how much to eat. The thermostat-like system shuts down when we sit around too much, but exercise keeps it working."

Our cravings for junk food aren't all bad. They're signs that the appestat is working. Bill Rodgers runs 120 to 150 miles a week, and at less than 130 pounds he doesn't have a very large fuel tank. To keep his energy up, his appestat tells him to take a 2 A.M. snack of milk and Oreos to power his morning run.

Sheehan himself follows only two diet rules: "First I must carry the least weight possible. Second I must have the most available energy possible."

He says, "The first must be accomplished without losing strength, the second without gaining weight."

This would be a hard line to walk if it were not for the automatic appestat.

"If you run," Sheehan notes, "the diet to use is one that maintains your proper weight, gives you energy for your training runs, and helps you race your best. It should also be a diet you enjoy. It might even include Twinkies."

FOOD FOR THOUGHT

GEORGE SHEEHAN FAVORS leanness but warns against extreme skinniness. He reports a study of ballet dancers who trained six to eight hours a day—far more than any runner. Their incidence of bone, muscle, and tendon injuries was as high as the casualty rate in any group of hard-working runners.

The researchers found that the dancers most prone to injuries were those on diets which stopped them short of 2000 calories a day. The healthiest were those who ate what their appetites requested.

The point: The body needs fuel from today's food for any kind of work, and it needs reserves—in the form of modest amounts of stored fat—for emergencies.

Athletic competition and training is an artificially created emergency. To keep handling it, we need plenty of food and some fat. Otherwise the body literally starts eating itself—breaking down its own muscle for fuel the way someone stranded in a mountain snowstorm might start burning the furniture.

Fat has long been thought to be the enemy of the fit. This has been accepted as true both for fat taken into the body as food and fat worn on the body as excess baggage. So runners have leaned toward leanness in what they eat and what they carry. We've often leaned too far.

Cholesterol was labeled as bad, so we aimed at the lowest intake and the lowest reading possible. But now science has cast doubt on the worth—even the safety—of these goals. Government researchers reported they had found no direct link between cholesterol readings and heart disease in people who had no other risk factors.

Cholesterol isn't even all bad. That has been the news from Dr. Peter Wood's research team at Stanford University. Wood has identified a "good cholesterol" made up of small, high-density particles which clean out the arteries like scouring powder rather than clogging them as the large globs of fat do.

The good news about this good cholesterol is that running helps produce it. In other words, a blood test may show a runner's total cholesterol reading to be no lower than Joe Snooze's. Yet on closer examination, the runner has a much greater percentage of self-cleaning particles. These don't lead to heart disease but help protect against it.

Dr. Thomas Bassler uses the term "friendly fats." He says they are not only one of a runner's best friends—they may save his life.

Bassler makes sometimes outrageous statements to get our attention. He's notorious for claiming that no runner who has completed a marathon has ever died of a heart attack. (He now qualifies that line several ways but still stands by the meat of it: that long-distance running provides near-perfect protection.)

To back up his claim, Bassler plays detective. He's a pathologist accustomed to studying dead bodies and autopsy reports. He asks to see the medical records of every runner suspected of being killed by a heart attack.

The doctor's faith in his own claims about the immunity of runners has been shaken in recent years by a flurry of sudden deaths. He has looked into dozens of similar cases: men in their 40s and even younger, lean non-smokers, running 40 to 50 miles a week or more, training for marathons, no history of heart problems.

A common thread running through their final days, says Bassler, has been a diet severely restricted in meats and most other fats. The doctor speculates that the unbalanced diet may lead to fatal disturbances in heartbeat patterns which he calls "nutritional arrhythmias." A certain amount of fat, he says, is vital to health—and even to heart safety.

Soda-Loading

GEORGE SHEEHAN CALLS himself a dietary agnostic. He says arguing with a runner about diet is like debating a true believer on religion. Both subjects offer lots of room for interpretation and opinion, and few absolute answers.

For all the writing and speaking the ubiquitous Dr. Sheehan has done, he has given little weight to dietary matters. He tells in one book of an exchange after a lecture in New York City. The first question was on diet.

"Well, I don't care much about diet," Sheehan said. "I don't talk about it."

The man asking the question persisted. He reminded the doctor that he had been advertised as saying a few words about diet.

"I just have," Sheehan said. Next subject . . .

But the subject won't go away that easily. So Sheehan is writing and speaking more about nutrition. His probing started, as most of his ideas do, with an experience of his own.

"I was standing in the kitchen area of the hospital, in full running gear, sipping grape juice," he writes. "My running companion was due in a few minutes. The juice was my final preparation for 10 miles over hills. Then the phone rang. He would be delayed. It would be another hour before we finally set out."

Weakness overtook Sheehan early in the run. He had to stop and walk.

"I had no alternative—except perhaps to stop and lie down," he says. "Fortunately we were passing a country club. So I suggested to my friend that we go in and get a drink. I had a large Coke. Within minutes, I started running again— quite tentatively at first, but soon with my usual energy. My legs felt strong. My head was clear. It was as if the entire episode had not occurred."

What had occurred, he knows now, was reactive hypoglycemia. The grape juice had triggered a quick rise in his blood sugar. The sugar level had peaked during the hour's wait for his partner, then had plunged before the run started. The Coke had boosted the blood sugar high enough to fuel Sheehan's run.

Dr. Sheehan, a maverick in his profession, doesn't blindly accept conventional wisdom. One bit of wisdom says that taking heavily sugared drinks while running is taboo. Sheehan's experience and later investigations showed otherwise.

He uncovered an old article in a medical journal. Dr. Samuel Levine wrote after the 1924 Boston Marathon, "There was a close correlation between the condition of the runner at the finish and the level of his blood sugar. Those with extremely low blood-sugar levels presented a picture of shock not unlike that produced by an overdose of insulin."

Dr. Levine suggested a half-century ago, "The adequate ingestion of carbohydrate would be of considerable benefit in preventing hypoglycemia and the accompanying symptoms of exhaustion."

Sheehan learned of another test, this one involving a dog named Joe. His master, researcher D. H. Dill, knew that other dogs tested on treadmill runs had rarely lasted more than 30 minutes. Joe was given a five-minute break every half-hour, during which he was fed sugar and water. The fox terrier ran for 17 hours and still wasn't exhausted when the test ended.

Letters to Sheehan from a friend in South Africa confirmed the results of these old studies. Dr. Timothy Noakes told George that low blood sugar is the forgotten disease of long-distance runners.

"South Africans are quite familiar with the effects of low blood sugar and the efficacy of sugar replacement," Sheehan says.

Runners from this country where the 56-mile Comrades' race is the most popular event have devised the Coke test.

Sheehan explains, "If a runner's exhaustion, incoordination or any other untoward symptoms are relieved within minutes by five to six ounces of Coke, they believe the problem is due to hypoglycemia."

One top runner collapsed in the Comrades', Dr. Noakes reported. No blood-sugar reading registered on a test tape. Within minutes of receiving a glucose solution, the runner was "coherent, cheerful, and eager to get moving."

Sheehan, the pragmatist, draws three lessons from all of this:

1. Don't take sugar 30 to 90 minutes before running. It may lead to the kind of grape-juice reaction that George experienced.
2. Sugar, taken in liquid form, may be the best antidote to the runner's low, if taken immediately before, during, or after a long training session or race.
3. Immediate carbohydrate reloading after a run may be more valuable than loading before it.

E

Exercises of Faith

George Sheehan tells this story. He is a physician, an internist by specialty. The party line in his trade is that vitamin supplements do a healthy person no good. If he takes more than the small amount of vitamins that he needs and gets naturally from foods, he flushes out the excess as "expensive urine."

Dr. Sheehan recalls going to a medical convention. One speaker talked about vitamins. He asked at the beginning, "How many of you believe in mega-doses of supplements and recommend them to your patients?"

Only a scattering of hands went up. The doctors who put them up looked embarrassed at being caught violating the party line.

"Okay," the speaker said, "now I want to know how many of *you* take extra vitamins and tell your own families to do the same."

Nearly every doctor in the house held up his hand.

"Just as I thought," said the man onstage. After admitting that he too gulped down a handful of pills each day, he told his colleagues, "We are like atheists who still go to church each Sunday—just in case we might be wrong in our non-belief."

Runners take another kind of supplement without really knowing why or believing in it totally. This is extra exercise in the form of stretching and strength-building training. The Sheehan tale applies here, either as told or in reverse. We either pay lip service to the exercises and don't do them, or we follow them religiously without truly believing.

Dr. Sheehan admits that he is part of the first crowd. He has preached extra exercise for years. One of his catch-phrases is, "Running does three things for you. Two of them are bad." The good one is that it makes you a faster, stronger, more efficient runner. But the bad results are muscle imbalances and inflexibility.

George's columns, books, and talks are filled with advice on stretching and strengthening. He devised the "Magic Six," a popular set of exercises.

And yet if you press him on the subject, he'll admit that he rarely does anything but run. He has shown onstage before large audiences that he can barely do a single bent-leg situp. He concedes that he can't bend over while standing and touch his toes.

This is an admission of guilt. George Sheehan is one of many runners who thinks he should start exercising—tomorrow. That tomorrow always stays a day away.

The doubters, like the doctors in the vitamin story, represent an equal and opposite crowd. They don't think this exercising does much good, and they sometimes wonder if it might do some harm. If they say anything positive, it is, "These exercises should be taken as a prescription item—only in small and proper doses, only to correct a specific weakness and only the exercises designed for that specific problem."

When pressed, though, these doubters may confess to superstition about exercises. They don't believe in them rationally, but are like the atheist who keeps going to church or the doubting doctor who keeps taking vitamins. Until all the evidence is in, they want to be sure they're not making a mistake.

They limit themselves to a few exercises—some for strength and some for stretch—taking perhaps five minutes total. This is enough to make them think they're safe but not so much that they risk harm.

Strengthening and Stretching

Evan Scott wavers between faith and doubt, but is a regular exerciser. "I don't like these exercises," he says, "but I would have the stomach muscles of an uncooked chicken and arms of toothpicks if I didn't do my few pushups and sit-ups each day. With the exercises, I have the strength of your average 10-year-old. This may not aid my running in the slightest. But it does let me carry out the garbage or mow the lawn without getting stiff.

"The effects of stretching are more obvious. Running is a tightener, and the few stretches I do seem to loosen me up. If I didn't stretch, I fear my leg muscles would grow so taut that they would pull apart like brittle guitar strings. This may not happen when I run, because that is just slow and straight-ahead movement. But put me in a touch football game or a one-on-one basketball shootout, and you could almost hear the tearing."

Scott says no one exercised the way runners do now in his days as a college athlete—"no one but sprinters, anyway, and we didn't count them as real runners. I could fit into a single hour all the time I spent strengthening and stretching during my first 10 years of running."

As George Sheehan notes, however, the longer a runner runs the *less fit* he becomes in terms of upper-body strength and lower-body flexibility. Scott started doing remedial stretches in the 1970s after a doctor (who was treating him for a knee injury) pointed out that he (Scott) couldn't reach past his knees on a toe-touch. He began strengthening a few years later when his son beat him at arm wrestling. The son was 14 years old at the time.

Scott's exercise routine evolved. "I added and dropped exercises according to their cost-benefit ratio," he says. "In other words, I didn't mind if they were a little bit unpleasant, if they helped in the long run. The ones that were just plain pain were the first to go."

> **Example:** the heels-over-head exercises called "the plow" by yogists. ("It strained me all the way from the upper neck to the lower back without seeming to do a bit of good. I dropped it early.")

> **Example:** the sitting, soles-of-feet-together, knees-out exercises called "the butterfly." ("It was too much for my tight groin to take. I got rid of this exercise, and the pain immediately waned.")

> **Example:** bounding in triple-jump fashion, featuring springing from the ankles and lifting high the knees. ("My achilles tendons took one hell of a beating, before I saw what I was doing to them and stopped it.")

The exercises Evan stayed with were the ones that proved themselves profitable. He says, "The profits have never been more than modest. But I do feel slightly better for doing the exercises and worse if I skip them for too many days. That's good enough evidence for me."

Scott's exercises boiled down to five which he does for about a minute each after most runs.

SIT-UPS. Flop down on the back on soft ground or a carpet. Bend the knees until they form a pyramid—feet together and flat on the floor, hollow gone from the lower back. Use the arms to help sit up all the way, then lace the hands behind the head while going back down. ("I've done sit-ups many other ways, but this is the only one I can manage without straining.") Do twenty of them.

BUTT STRETCHES. Sit cross-legged on the floor after the last sit-up. From this Indian-style position, bend as far forward and reach as far out as possible. Hold for 10 to 30 seconds. Then add a twist by extending one leg straight out and cradling the bent knee of the other. Pull the bent leg toward the straight-legged side while twisting the upper body the opposite way. ("Trying to translate exercises from movement into words is as hard as making sense of Swahili.") Reverse the action by cradling the other knee. Spend only about a minute on this set of exercises.

PUSHUPS. Nothing fancy. Just stretch out with face to the ground and touch the nose to the surface twenty times. Keep the back straight—no cheating.

HAMSTRING STRETCHES. Stand up and spread the legs to about shoulder width apart. Turn one foot out to a right angle. While still facing forward with hands laced behind the head, bend sideways in the direction of the out-turned foot until the elbow touches the knee. Hold for long seconds. Then go into the second stage by turning in that direction, bending the knee and reaching out along the ground as far as possible that way. Repeat these stretches from the other side.

CALF STRETCHES. Put one foot in front of the other, as if getting ready to start a sprint race. Bend down on one knee, placing the other heel about a hand's width in front of it. Then, with the hands on the floor for balance, stand up. In phase two, extend the position by spreading the legs farther

apart and thrusting forward as if fencing. R.
other side.

Scott concludes that "some of my reasons for t.
exercise have nothing to do with how it may or n.   .not
affect my running health and performance. I sometimes
think of it as a post-run ritual. It is doing a certain thing, in
a certain way, at a certain time, for a certain period of time
each day, with the thought that it achieves some higher
purpose."

More often, he views the exercising simply as a superstitious act of no practical value. "But for the same reasons that
I am wary of Friday the 13th and I detour around cats with
black coats, I keep exercising—just to be sure."

PLAYING THE EDGE

WHETHER YOU TAKE extra exercise or not, you have to credit
the stretchers with a theory that applies to all types of training. They say to make friends with ourselves, to coax out the
benefits of the exercise instead of trying to beat them out, to
listen to the body's rhythms instead of trying to blot out its
screams.

Ian Jackson is the "Kenneth Cooper of Stretching." Jackson's *Yoga and the Athlete* was every bit as revolutionary a
book, despite its smaller sales, as Cooper's first *Aerobics* text.
Cooper said the way to train most effectively is to work
steadily and gently, not briefly and violently. Jackson wrote
much the same about stretching exercises.

His yoga book was packaged and promoted as how-to information. It chronicles one man's journey away from the
whip-into-shape mentality that dominates athletics, and to
the friendlier methods of the Eastern activity.

Jackson noted the key phrase in yoga: "Play the edge." This concept makes it as different from traditional calisthenics as LSD running is from interval training. Ian said that the violent stretching of calisthenics tries to crash pain barriers, while yoga nudges them until they move quietly out of the way.

He gave the example of two ways to do a simple toe-touch from a standing position. A runner from the pain-equals-gain school bends down quickly. Momentum carries his fingertips to the ground before a reflex action pulls them up again. He has reached way down, but has he done himself any good? Researchers think not. They say the muscles rebel against this treatment, tightening rather than loosening. This sudden movement may even *cause* injury.

The yoga approach is to stretch carefully to the point of discomfort, back off slightly, then hold at that point for a few seconds. The first thing you notice is that you ease farther down without really trying. You notice after a few weeks of stretching this way that the edge has moved to a point you could earlier reach only with great pain. You now stretch to it comfortably.

"Playing the edge" means finding that invisible, ever-shifting line between comfort and discomfort. If you never nudge it, you never move it. If you push it too hard, it breaks you. Whatever your exercise is, this rule applies.

F

Faster, Easier

CURES FOR "SPEEDOPHOBIA"

WE LISTEN WITH ONLY HALF AN EAR to the true experts and listen too closely to their interpreters. Two experts on high-mileage, low-intensity training have been Arthur Lydiard and Ernst van Aaken. We assumed because of their emphasis that they preached *only* this. They didn't. Both recommended carefully measured doses of speed. Lydiard's runners took it all at once during their brief "sharpening" periods. Van Aaken, a doctor, prescribed it daily, year-round.

Interpreters have taken half of what Lydiard and van Aaken said and have run to extremes with it. The revisionists have said that all distance running is pleasant, and you can't take too much of it; all speed hurts and is to be avoided.

"Speedophobia" has limited a generation of runners as a result. If you won't do speedwork because you only think of it as fast time-trials and hard interval sessions on the track, you have this phobia. Here are two antidotes, ways to grow faster without taking speedwork to its extreme.

RACE MORE. Bob Deines, then 21 years old, missed the 1968 Olympic Marathon team by one place. He said he did no speed training without a gun held to his head, and he hadn't run under the gun for years.

"Regular racing helps keep me sharp," Bob said. "I think that two or three races are sufficient to recover any lost sharpness without any speed training. It works out to an almost exact formula with me. I'm usually a little sluggish in my first fast race. It may take 4:27 to run a mile. But within a week or two, it's sure to be 4:17. The 10-second (per mile) improvement seems to be pretty standard."

Race yourself to racing sharpness, he advised. It's the most specific way to learn to run hard. The excitement factor at races makes you push harder than you ever would in practice. Race up to your full quota of quality work, giving special attention to the races at the short end of your range, and you need no special speed training.

This advice assumes, however, that your area's racing program supplies the right number of races, at the right distances, at the right times. Most programs aren't this perfect, so you must improvise.

SIMULATE. If you don't have enough real races available, make up your own events. Simulate racing by running one of your shorter distances for time at full race pace. Instead of running it steadily, break it into several equal parts. Stop the watch and walk for a few minutes between segments, while taking only an overall running time.

For instance, a five-minute miler might run 75-second quarters with five-minute walks separating them. This mimics the pace and excitement of the race without adding the stress loads of either conventional speedwork or full-scale racing.

KEEPING TRACK OF PROGRESS

PROGRESS DOESN'T FOLLOW a straight upward course—it sometimes runs in a circle. Don Elliott spent more than half of his life running a big circle leading back to where he had started.

Elliott didn't dread his 40th birthday, which was less than a year away, as a bridge to cross on the inevitable trip into middle age. Rather, he welcomed that day as an opening into a second childhood. Time drew him back to the tracks of his youth. What time had taken away in speed, it had returned in a clear understanding of all the good things he'd done blindly 20 years earlier.

At 40, the runner becomes a Master. In one day, he goes from being the oldest of the young to the youngest of the old. Many of the inequities of age are wiped away. The new Master becomes like a high-school freshman again—the new kid on the track—only this time with all the training and experience that was lacking in the first childhood. Age is now an asset.

At 39, Elliott was catching glimpses of the runner he once had been and might again become. Not that illusions of 4:18 miles danced in his head. He simply saw opportunity that he hadn't known in years: the chance to race on the track without being eaten alive by hungry kids.

Old trackmen never die; they just run out of races. Don's had run out when college ended, and he had gone to the roads by default. There had been no place else to race. But progress had changed both track and road racing.

He once had liked the roads for what they *didn't* offer. They had lacked the crowds and the win-at-any-cost pressure of track meets. But now the road races were overcrowded. A worship-the-winner attitude had crept in.

Masters track, which was born and had matured since Don

had left college, offered the kinds of comfortable feelings that the roads had given him 15 years before.

"I'm drawn back to the track because I don't care to follow crowds," Elliott says. "But I also come back because this is where I belong. The track is the truest measure of a runner. Every road course is different, but every track is the same. It has two straightaways and two turns—no hills, no aiding wind, no way to get lost, no chance for mismeasurement, no place to hide. The times that really mean something are made on the track. Self-testing at its best occurs here."

Track racing is the purest test of who Elliott is, he says. "I'm not now and never have been a marathoner. While I've run lots of marathons and other road distances, I've never raced them as a specialty. I'm a sprinter by temperament, a sprinter by build, by heredity, by background—a sprinter by choice."

As a high-school freshman with no specific training for sprinting, Don had run 100 yards on a lumpy grass field in 11 seconds flat. That isn't world-class speed, but not bad for a boy who'd never been timed before. He would later drop his 100 time to 10.6 (still over rough grass), his quarter-mile to 52 seconds (in an empty stadium during a Sunday workout), and his half-mile to 1:55 (again in a time-trial).

He says, "Maybe I missed my true calling by not aiming at distances below a mile. I chose the mile because it was then, as it still is, the sexiest race. My speed still served me well there and on through 10,000 meters—the track distances, in other words. As I approach my second childhood, I'm drawn back to those distances that I ran well then without knowing why. This time, I know why."

Runners in small high schools like Don Elliott's didn't train in the 1950s. They started racing several times a week after basketball season ended, then raced themselves into shape by the end of the track season. They weren't expected to run again until the next spring.

With no training worthy of the name, Don made the state

meet as a freshman. This first taste of success in any sport built his appetite for more the next year. He would get a jump on that season by running through the winter.

"I had no coaching, no advice to read, no one to race me into shape at this time of year," he recalls. "I had only my instincts. They directed me to the countryside, where I looped a four-mile section of land or two. These runs took 30 to 60 comfortably paced minutes. I wasn't trying to strain myself, only to pass the time until racing started again. In season, I simply mixed a weekly race or two into this easy distance running."

This combination worked. Elliott won several state high-school titles—in times that he would improve only marginally, if at all, under harder and more sophisticated training schemes. Because he didn't know what he had then, he lost it. He tried to improve on perfection, first by swinging too far in the direction of speedwork, then too far toward distance.

This is not just Elliott's story but the story of training trends over the last 20 years. What might be called progress is nothing more than regular pendulum swings back and forth from one form of self-destruction to another. The lesson from the last 20 years has been that too much of any-thing—speed or distance—equals nothing.

As Don Elliott completes the great circuit back to where he started, he runs again much as he did then—and knows that territory for the first time.

"I run the same 30 to 60 minutes a day that I did then— only now I know this is the ideal running time and don't try to improve on it," he says. "I race the same 10,000-and-below distances as before—but now the racing is more of a game than a serious sport. I *play* at racing instead of working at it, because long-term running is now more important than im-mediate racing goals."

One Saturday morning, he went to the track to race a mile. He wanted only to do it in less than five minutes. This wasn't a good time by his old standards, but not bad for a man of 39 who averaged *eight*-minute miles day by day.

He says, "I felt I was coming home after too long on the road. Nine months had passed since I'd raced any distance on the track, nine *years* since that distance had been a mile. But you don't forget how to race here. You may feel a little rusty, but the old moves are still there—automatic, instinctive.

"As I raced, I saw no one on the track with me and no one in the stands. I was aware only of being surrounded by ghosts of runners and crowds past. Their footsteps and shouts echoed through the empty stadium."

Don's time of 4:55 would have been his fastest since the 1960s, except that he cheated. Oh, he raced four laps around the quarter-mile track in the total time listed. But that mile really took almost 20 minutes. He walked a five-minute lap after each fast quarter.

This was his way of playing at racing, of filling the gaps between true races. This was less than all-out racing and more than interval training. It had some of the violence of racing but not too much of it to handle alone. It had more meaning than intervals and less of their meaningless repetition.

Such tests can be run at any distance and with any com-bination of work and recovery periods. They simulate the sensations of racing without matching the stress loads. They tell you what you can and can't expect when you do race. They remind a runner like Don Elliott of how things were when he really raced, and how they might be again in his second childhood.

Speeding without Bleeding

If you occasionally want to run faster than normal—but don't very often want the discomforts and risks of true rac-ing, this plan is for you:

1. *Save the hard work for races, when it counts.* Never run anywhere near full racing distance at full race pace when there isn't a crowd around to help.
2. *Run regular test races in lieu of real ones.* Match many of the experiences of racing, but not its brutality. Treat these tests as intermediate steps between the ease of everyday runs and the effort of races.
3. *Learn finesse.* Practice the skill of running faster than usual. Learn to stretch out for more speed without straining.
4. *Rehearse the race.* With the one exception of the walking breaks, treat it like a real race. Run on a track or an accurately measured course. Dress as in racing. Warm up and cool down well.
5. *Choose a distance shorter* than your daily runs, probably one taking less than 30 minutes. Run it at least a minute a mile faster than your usual pace.
6. *Divide the distance into four equal parts.* Run each part as if you were racing. Time them precisely.
7. *Walk for about five minutes between the parts.* Stop the watch during the rest periods (simply estimate their length), and start it again as you resume running at the point where you had stopped.
8. *Time the running portion of the test as a whole,* as if there were no breaks. Record the total time and the "splits."
9. *Test yourself no more than once a week.* Do no testing within a week either side of a true race (or longer afterward if the distance is more than 10 kilometers).
10. *Abort the planned test race if you feel any symptoms of injury before or during the session.* Never run anything that might turn a small problem into a big one.

G

Going Beyond

THE MOST FROM THE LEAST

EXPERIENCE IS THE best laboratory. A runner somewhere usually discovers that something works before a scientist confirms that it might.

A copy of notes which came to *Running* magazine illustrate that point. The paper went by the ponderous title of "Preliminary Investigation into the Adaptability of the Osler System to Marathon Running for Lightly Trained Individuals." It might have been called "How to Survive a Marathon without Really Training" or "A Marathon on Five Miles a Day."

The notes weren't intended for publication, and their authors only agreed to let the magazine quote from them if the editors gave adequate warning that this was a preliminary study and if they didn't mention the authors' names. The same ground rules apply here.

Fair enough. We'll call them McCreary, Groves, and

44

Wright of the University of the Roads. They want it made clear that they have only formulated a hypothesis which requires extensive further testing among large groups of runners operating under controlled conditions.

These men use the ideas of two ultramarathoners, Ken Young and Tom Osler, as their takeoff point. The runners learned through their own experience how far they could push the limits of distance.

Young developed the now widely accepted collapse-point theory. It states that a person can run to about three times his average daily training distance before slowing dramatically, or "hitting the wall" in runner jargon. This means a marathoner-to-be tries to average at least 8.7 miles a day for two months to avoid "collapsing."

Some runners get by on less weekly mileage than the 60 or so which Young recommends. However, they do it by taking frequent long runs of 20 miles and more, and by running little between them.

Tom Osler accepts Young's formula but adds that it can be varied. A runner, Osler says, can double the distance that the collapse-point theory indicates is the limit. Osler offers two tricks:

1. *Take caffeinated, sugared drinks as fuel before and during the run.*
2. *Take frequent, short walking breaks to hold off fatigue.*

Osler devised this system to use himself when he wanted to graduate from marathons to 50-mile, 100-mile, and longer races without taking on correspondingly more training.

The University of the Roads experimenters wondered, "Would this same system apply to lightly trained runners who want to complete standard marathons which, by normal standards, would be outside their reach?"

They did a feasibility study on a single runner. They describe him as "a 37-year-old male with extensive marathon-

ing experience in the past, but nothing approaching this distance for the previous 18 months. He had taken no runs or
races longer than an hour in duration for nearly a year. He
averaged five to six miles a day, which should have limited
him to 15 to 18 miles using the Young formula. This test
was made even more rigorous by the fact that the marathon
he chose would cross a 2000-foot mountain ridge."

The subject and the testers agreed that his procedure
would be:

· Drinking a Dr. Pepper (containing sugar and caffeine) at the start and at halfway, and taking only water
at the aid stations located every two-and-a-half miles. It was
impractical to give a special drink more than once during
the marathon.

· Walking an average of one minute per mile while
drinking, or two to three minutes at each aid station. Otherwise he would run at his natural pace of about eight-
minute miles. The projected total time was four hours—a
3:30 marathon plus a half-hour of break time.

The subject did much better than that: a 3:35 total and
3:10 of running time. He told the observers afterward, "No
one promised it would be easy, and it wasn't. Oh, it went as
easily as any of my marathons had when I'd trained for them.
But 'easy' is a relative term. Near the end, I cramped in the
upper legs—same as always. I thought about stopping completely—same as always.

"And no one said it would be fast. It wasn't. I did it almost
a half-hour faster than expected, but this marathon still set
a 'PW' (personal worst) by 11 minutes. I survived, though—
survived the distance itself and survived to walk away from
it and run the next day."

The cost of this system is a minute per mile added to the
time. The reward is survival. Running this way wouldn't be
of much interest to a 10-plus-mile-a-day trainer or to anyone

chasing a record. But it deserves wider testing among runners who want to get the most from the least.

Go Longer by Stopping

IF YOU CAN RACE A MARATHON, you can finish a 50-mile run. This doesn't mean you might be able to finish the 50 if you train twice as much as you did for the marathon. It means the same training can take you twice as far as you've gone before—twice the distance the "collapse-point" theory says you're able to run. If you have raced a marathon, you are ready *now* for a 50.

Fifty miles is where ultramarathoning truly begins, say two runners who should know.

Tom Osler, one of the few Americans to have covered more than 200 miles in 48 hours, writes in his *Serious Runner's Handbook*, "I like to think of 50 kilometers (31.1 miles) as merely a long marathon. The shortest ultramarathon worthy of the name is the 50-miler."

Nick Marshall, a veteran of 100-mile races, agrees. He says in *The Complete Marathoner*, "Fifty kilometers, while by definition an 'ultra,' has more in common with the standard marathon than it does with these longer events. Unfortunately there are currently no other intermediate steps on the way to 50 miles. Therefore the aspiring ultra runner is typically confronted with a quantum leap from 26 to 50 miles."

Fifty-mile runs should be the first container to catch the overflow from marathoning. People who have sucked the challenge out of that race and now are annoyed by its crowds should be spilling into this ultra.

But Osler notes, "In spite of the tremendous growth that has been seen in the marathon and shorter distances in recent years, the ultramarathons fail to attract entrants. For every 100 who finish the marathon, only one will finish 50 miles."

That's because so few runners try the 50. Osler's figures probably are conservative. The U.S. has close to 100,000 marathoners but fewer than 1000 finishers of runs 50 miles and up. However, the fact that so few runners have been willing to try these distances doesn't change the fact that thousands of us are more able than we think.

South Africans aren't specially bred for ultramarathoning, yet the 56-mile Comrades run is their "Boston." Almost 3000 of them try it each year. Translating this into American population terms (we have 10 times more people), the national 50-mile championship race would need 30,000 people to match it. This most important of U.S. 50-mile runs usually has a field of a few dozen.

This comparison is made not to show how small our ultramarathoning population is now, but rather to show what is possible when runners raise their distance sights. The South Africans have set their goal at 56 miles for more than half a century, and the distance doesn't scare them.

By contrast, large numbers of Americans have only started marathoning in the last decade. The gulf between the marathon and the ultras now looks as wide as the one between track distances and 26 miles seemed in the 1960s. We successfully crossed that gulf, so a mass jump to 50 miles could happen, given the right combination of conditions: heroes to show what the best of us can do and models to show what any of us can do; teachers who have done it and can tell us exactly what to do; places to do it with the competition and support of runners like us.

HEROES AND MODELS. Park Barner kept going until he ran out of competition. As a high-school miler, he was slow; he ran 5:45. His first marathon took more than five hours, and even now about a thousand runners a year do better than his fastest time in the 2:30s.

Barner gets more successful at 50 miles but still isn't close to record time. At twice that distance, he has held the American record, but a much younger Jose Cortez ran a faster time on the roads, and a much older Ted Corbitt went almost as fast as Park on the track.

Apparently 100 miles of running only begins to warm Barner up. He doesn't leave everyone else behind until he goes for 24 hours or more. In 1978, he broke the one-day run record by almost 20 miles and said after finishing his 152.9 miles, "I could have gone 300."

Corbitt, Cortez, and 50-milers like Bob Deines were cult figures whose long runs were reported to just a few followers · of this arcane branch of the sport. However, Barner achieved hero status when his feats were certified in *Sports Illustrated*. Thousands of long-distance runners now know his story. Hundreds may want to imitate him.

They'll soon realize that isn't possible. There may be only one Park Barner. But there can be other Rich Benyos. Benyo's running means more to most of us than Barner's, because Rich shows what anyone might be capable of doing.

When Benyo walked into the *Runner's World* magazine office to apply for a job in 1977, he wore a pinkish double-knit suit that didn't hide what was hanging over his white belt. His weight had gone up by 50 pounds since he'd quit running in college. He'd only recently decided to correct that.

By 1978, Benyo was skinny again and running marathons. He did them at the rate of one a month through that spring and summer. When this distance no longer satisfied him, he tried 50 miles. He failed the first time, failed again the second—both of these on the track.

Rich's third 50 was at Cow Mountain. He called it "the only totally vertical cross-country run I've taken in my life." He finished.

TEACHERS AND TRICKS. Conventional training wisdom states that you must average one-third of the racing distance each day to finish without hitting a wall. Using this formula, a

50-miler needs to go 17 miles a day with frequent long runs into the 30s.

Right there, we have a reason why so few people try ultras. The training time and effort are too great. But wait—there are shortcuts. These come from Tom Osler and Nick Marshall. As noted, they are accomplished ultramarathon racers, but they contribute even more as teachers of the less gifted and less serious. Both of them tell us lightly trained runners to treat the 50 quite differently from any race we've run before.

Osler says of his tricks—stopping often for rest breaks and drinking gallons of heavily sugared mixes—"It has been my experience that any runner who has not tried these two techniques will be able to double the longest distance he has ever covered on foot without any additional training."

Independently, Marshall gives the same advice: "Include some preplanned walking along the way. Walking breaks will make it much easier on the body, instill calm in the mind, and not really penalize you as much as you'd think. It is a fact of ultramarathoning that most entrants will slow considerably anyway, and many will have to walk at some point in the event. Voluntary walks are not a blow to morale like ones forced upon you by a rebelling body. They keep you fresh."

What might have been an intolerably long race becomes a manageable interval workout.

RACES AND RUNNERS. Each year, the United States supports more than 300 marathons. The country has about one-tenth that many ultras. The second total may seem small by comparison, but the country didn't yet have this many standard 26-milers as recently as 1970.

There are 24-hour runs on each coast, 100-milers in several different places, many more races of 100 kilometers and more than a dozen 50-milers. We have events now, begging to be filled.

The biggest, the John F. Kennedy 50-Mile, which is over mountainous terrain in Maryland, doesn't even call itself a race. It's a "Run/Hike." Traditionally it attracts several hundred people, and the number of finishers is by far the highest in U.S. ultras. What isn't clear is how many of those are hikers and what percentage of walking turns a run into a hike.

There's no point in quibbling over definitions. One fact is clear from the JFK experience: An event grows quickly when the emphasis is taken away from racing, when entrants know it's okay for them to take it slowly and do some walking.

An even more extreme example of this is the Western States 100-Mile. It crosses the High Sierra range in California, climbing 17,000 feet in all. No one is going to hurry this one, and some walking is mandatory. Yet the entry limit of 250 is reached a year in advance.

This tells us that runners aren't looking for an easy ultra, only one they can do without hurrying. Sustained speed seems to frighten away more people than do distance and terrain.

Experiment in Break-Taking

Before Park Barner and Rich Benyo, before Tom Osler and Nick Marshall, before the JFK 50 and the Western States 100, Kenneth Crutchlow was the model, and the 100-mile run at Rocklin, California, was the opportunity.

Crutchlow is English. His adventures have included hitch-hiking around the world, racing a ship to Alaska on a bicycle and relay-running from the floor of Death Valley to the peak of Mt. Whitney. He ran from Los Angeles to San Francisco in 1971, covering the 550 miles in 10 days. He did this without training.

"I don't plan these things," Crutchlow said then. "That's half the fun, going into them unprepared. This is why I can't train. If I had to do this kind of preparation, it would become a bit of a bore. Unlike marathoners who run every day, I don't know my capabilities. I'm always surprising myself with what I'm able to do."

But people don't run 55 miles day after day on spirit alone. What was Ken's secret for easing the load of miles?

"Five-mile bursts," he said. "That's how I ran it—five miles at a time with a bit of rest between the runs. I spread the running out over the whole bloody day. Never would have made it otherwise."

What was good enough for untrained Crutchlow seemed good enough for a mildly trained runner who recounts his experience with a 100-mile run attempted a few weeks after talking with Crutchlow in 1971:

"I started by running five miles at a time, carrying that through 50 miles. The breaks were 10 to 15 minutes, with longer stops after 25 and 50 miles. At that point, I dropped down to 2½-mile runs—one lap of the course—with 10-minute breaks between.

"By then, it was past midnight. The lights in the homes of Rocklin had gone out. Four other runners were still on the course somewhere, but I couldn't see them. I'd never felt so desperately alone. Nothing I'd ever done seemed quite so senseless as running these laps by myself in the dark after I'd already done so many.

"I sat down for my break after finishing the 70th mile and couldn't get back up. The thought of going on was too depressing. I shouted weakly to the scorer to mark me out.

"I was very tired *of* running. But to my surprise, I wasn't at all tired *from* it—even after 14 hours and 2½ times more distance than I'd ever run. Ken Crutchlow was right. By taking long runs in small bites, physical fatigue can be held off all day. Mental fatigue was a problem that Ken solved better than I did."

H

Healthy and Happy

Preventive "Proof-Running"

As the woman was introduced to the running magazine editor, the first thing she said after the "hellos" and "nice-to-meet-you's" passed between them was, "I must say, you certainly let a lot of typographical errors slip by you."

The editor had no defense. All he could do was shrug and say, "Everyone makes mistakes, but most people can bury theirs. The trouble with mine is that they're so visible. I have thousands of readers ready to tell me how sloppy I am."

His magazine once surveyed a random group of about 1000 subscribers. The largest number of complaints was directed at the quality of the proofreading.

"The proofreading in your publication is not very thorough—many errors," one reader said.

Another ordered, "Proofread! Way too many unsightly typos in each issue."

"The complaints were justified," the editor admits.

"There is no excuse for mistakes of this kind in a profession-
ally edited journal. As the magazine added staff, the proofing
improved. But errors still managed to get into print because
of the nature of the work, and the complaints still came in
because of the nature of readers who delight in catching
editors with their pencils down.

"I don't say this as a plea for patience and understanding.
Proofreading is my problem. But it relates to a problem all
of us have when we run. That's the matter of correcting little
mistakes at the source, before they have gone too far or
grown too large to solve."

Proofreading an article involves stopping errors before
they get into print. The better proofing an editor does, the
less it's noticed. He may catch 99 of 100 flubs, but the one
that slips through to the readers is the one that makes him
a bad proofreader. Once the errors go public, they're easy to
see but impossible to correct.

Running works the same way. Preventive medicine might
be called "proof-running." That means catching injuries and
illnesses before they happen. Proof-running requires a close
reading of your own signs and reactions. It's a quiet job and,
like proofreading, is noticed least when it is done best. Physical breakdowns, once they happen, are easy to see but hard
to treat.

The message is to stay alert. Weed out errors while they
still are small and before anyone else is able to notice them—
advice too easy to give and so hard to follow.

Every longtime runner's logbook is littered with preventable injuries and illnesses. These weren't accidents any more
than were the typos, because accidents happen by chance.
These mistakes follow a visible pattern: trouble, resolving
not to let it happen again, forgetting the resolution, overcon-
fidence in abilities or inattention to warnings, more trouble.

When someone sets out to practice prevention—preventing printing errors, as an editor must do to keep working, or
preventing the erosion of health, which we all must do to

keep running—he can judge the results most clearly by his mistakes.

No one praises an editor for correcting 99 of every 100 typos before they reached print. No one notices that nine out of every ten running days were painless. Only the failures are highly visible in any kind of preventive work. No matter how many errors you catch, you still get nailed for the one that got away. And one always gets away because cleaning things up works that way.

Imagine that you're renovating an old house. Trash and dirt are everywhere. You quickly push out the big pieces by hand. Each step after that gets more exacting—shovel, broom, mop, and, finally, dust rag. The last and smallest traces of dirt are the hardest to wipe away. The same is true in running cleanup work.

Another reason why proofing is discouraging is that second-guessing always comes easier than original effort. As you read magazines and books, typographical errors jump out, catching your eye. You say to yourself, "It's so obvious. Why didn't anyone catch that?"

Likewise, when you listen to the sad story of a runner who has broken down physically or psychologically, you think, "That wouldn't have happened if he'd just read the warning signs and made corrections soon enough."

How easy it is to tell someone else what went wrong. How hard it is to do what's right for yourself.

THE WARNING SIGNS

TOM OSLER HAS HAD IT BOTH WAYS—long and fast. With over a quarter-century career, he has raced nearly 800 times. He won three national long-distance championships in the 1960s. This experience, combined with the analytical talent of a scientist (he's a college mathematics professor in New Jersey), makes Osler a man worth listening to.

He says of his hundreds of races, "I can't imagine one of these that did my health any good. Racing is simply too hard to be placed in the healthful-exercise category."

His races are "an indirect blessing," he says. "If it were not for my interest in racing, I probably would have abandoned my training runs long ago. These runs have been an enormous boon to my general well-being, both physical and mental."

Many years ago, Osler listed in *The Conditioning of Distance Runners* a set of warning signs that protect his health and performance. These physical and mental symptoms of overstress tell him when to slam on his brakes and avoid all racing and race-like training until the road clears.

The 10 surest signs of too much stress, adapted from Tom's original list are:

1. Resting pulse rate significantly higher than normal when taken first thing in the morning.
2. Difficulty falling asleep and staying asleep.
3. Cold sores in and around the mouth, and other skin eruptions in non-adolescents.
4. Any symptoms of a cold or the flu—sniffles, sore throat, or fever.
5. Swollen, tender glands in the neck, groin, or underarms—signs that the body is fighting infection.
6. Labored breathing during the mild exertion of daily running.
7. Dizziness or nausea before, during, or after running.
8. Clumsiness—for instance, tripping or kicking yourself during a run over rather smooth ground.
9. Any muscle or tendon pain or stiffness that remains after the first few minutes of a run.
10. Feelings of dread or depression before a race, without the usual balance of excitement.

Treat each of these signs as a mild early warning that you're racing toward a crash.

Pressure Points

DR. JOAN ULLYOT TELLS of a visit with Arthur Lydiard in New Zealand. The famed coach was recovering from knee surgery and the first serious case of the flu in his 60-plus years. The two physical ailments probably weren't coincidental. The stress of his operation may have lowered his defenses against the virus.

A growing number of physicians now believe that we don't "catch" diseases like the flu and colds; they catch us. These bugs attack constantly, but only gain a foothold when excessive stress pokes holes in our natural immunity.

The connection between stress and illness is strong. We also know that specific stresses, such as running too fast or too far, cause injuries. A researcher in California now offers the theory that stresses apparently unrelated to training and racing loads may also lead to running injuries. For instance, a runner develops crippling sciatica while suffering through a divorce.

Walt Schafer believes such outside traumas often open the path to physical breakdowns. Schafer, a three-decade runner himself, is a sociology professor and director of a stress-management center.

He writes in his book *Stress, Distress and Growth*, "Drs. Thomas H. Holmes and Richard H. Rahe developed a scale for measuring stresses associated with 43 life events. On the basis of their research with thousands of people from all walks of life, they report that a person scoring less than 150 on this scale has only a 37-percent chance of becoming ill during the next two years. A score of 150 to 300 raises the odds of illness to 51 percent, and a 300-plus score means you have an 80-percent chance of becoming seriously ill."

The stressful life events range from death of a spouse, 100 points, and divorce, 73, down to a minor violation of the law, 11 points. Schafer thinks the effects are felt as injuries as well as illnesses.

To test this theory, he sent questionnaires to more than 1200 runnners. Of the 572 answering, the typical one was married, employed full time, a runner for four years, and currently averaging 30 miles weekly.

Schafer's preliminary findings:

> • "The higher the life-change score for the past year, the *greater number of running injuries* during the past three months, the *more days of running missed* during the past three months due to running injuries, and the *more days of running reduced* during the past three months due to running injuries."
> • The results were the same when Schafer examined the question, "Does the risk of running injuries increase when runners, for whatever reason, experience higher-than-usual personal stress during the past three months?"
> • He also found a direct link between injuries and chronic "Type-A behavior," which he defines as "a pattern of time urgency, intense drive to success, impatience and hostility."

The conclusion: Whenever overall stress levels climb dangerously, lower the ones over which you have control. Running is one of those. The researcher suggests, "Keep running during periods of high stress, but run with moderation and sensitivity to early warning signs of injury and illness. Back off in speed or distance when needed."

Schafer manages his own running stress well, after going the whole high-mileage/hard-marathon/heavy-injury route for many years.

He says, "Since 1980, I have run probably no more than

35 to 40 miles per week, with one fairly intense midweek workout and an occasional moderate speed workout. This is about 50 percent of previous years in distance and with fewer hard days along the way.

"Yet I have been able to nearly match several of my best times of the past decade (including a 10:10 two-mile and 15:38 three-mile after his 40th birthday). The less my hard training, the better I feel and the fewer my injuries."

Much of what he had done before in the name of training may have been straining.

I

Injuries and Illnesses

Down for Repairs

Given the luxury of a backward look, Paul Stevens sees that he worried for nothing. The injury wasn't as serious as it had looked in his first moments of pain and panic.

"In all of the achilles problems I've had," he says, "I can't remember a tendon ever going out—as this one did—in mid-race. One minute, I cruised along comfortably at a bit under six-minute miles. The next minute, I couldn't carry my own weight."

His first thought was, "Uh, oh! The big one!" Every runner fears a final, permanently crippling injury—his doomsday. Never mind that Stevens had run in 300 consecutive months and that no injury had been final yet. He was still sure a big one waited to strike him down sometime.

The physical pain of most running injuries doesn't amount to much, hurting less than an average headache or toothache. Doubt and fear are the runner's most crippling symptoms. The pain comes from not being able to run normally and not knowing when or if he or she ever will again.

Paul says, "I used to get tough with myself for being doubting and fearful. I would refuse to admit that I had a problem and would run as if I weren't hurt—thereby delaying the healing at best and hurting even more at worst."

He acted like the restless gardener who Jock Semple once described. Semple, best known as a fiesty Boston Marathon official, works as a physical therapist. Many of his patients are injured athletes—a growing number of them runners.

Semple gives his time freely to the running wounded, while complaining, "These runners are like gardeners who pull up their young carrots to see if they're growing." That stops the growth. Likewise, runners test their injuries to see how they are healing. This stops the healing.

"I can't count how many times I have reversed the healing process this way," says Stevens. "And still, hard as I've tried to injure myself permanently, I've always gotten better. The big injury has stayed away from my door."

Maybe that's one reason he has grown a little more patient. He knows now that hardly any problem lasts forever. And almost everything gets better quicker if he backs off and doesn't challenge any pain barriers.

As soon as Paul was injured this time, he put an emergency plan into action. His plan takes a middle course between running through pain and complete rest. If he can't run all the way, he walks or mixes walking and easy running. If he can't walk, he bikes or swims.

"I spend the same time—about an hour a day—at these substitutes as I would running. This isn't an attempt to match the exercise benefits I would get from a run. I don't worry about losing fitness. What I have spent years building up is not going to disappear in a few days.

"I stick with my hour a day workout to keep the *habit* alive. Not that it would die within a few days, either, but I would feel like the sun hadn't come up on any day when I couldn't do something active."

The recovery plan works through five stages:

1. *Biking or swimming.* These activities take nearly all of the pressure off of most injuries while still giving steady workouts. They make a runner feel he still has control over himself.
2. *Walking.* Start it as soon as it's possible to move around without limping, and continue as long as the pain doesn't increase. (These two limitations apply at all stages.)
3. *Walking mixed with running.* As the walks get too easy, add "intervals" of slow running—as little as one minute in five at first, then gradually building up the amounts of running until reaching . . .
4. *Running mixed with walking.* The balance tips in favor of the runs, but keep inserting brief walks at this stage when steady pressure can't yet be tolerated.
5. *Running again.* Approach it cautiously for a while, a little slower than normal, and with no long runs or races until the usual runs can be handled without having to retreat the next day to a lower stage.

With the latest injury, Paul Stevens raced through the recovery stages without pulling up any carrots or experiencing any withdrawal symptoms.

> • *First day*—limping badly after hurting the tendon in a race.
> • *Second day*—could hardly put weight on the damaged foot; rode a bike a hard 50 minutes and stayed off the foot as much as possible the rest of the day.
> • *Third day*—much better; walked 45 minutes without limping.
> • *Fourth day*—better yet; ran 30 minutes in intervals of 10 with five-minute walks between.
> • *Fifth day*—normal run except for its slower-than-usual pace; needed 50 minutes to circle a "45-minute" course.

Stevens adds, "While taking care of the foot, I ignored my head. It caught cold. That wasn't so bad, though, because it gave me an excuse to say here that the recovery plan applies to illnesses as well as injuries."

Fever and coughing replace inflammation and limping as the warning signs. But the steps back to health go in the same direction no matter what has gone wrong.

WATERED-DOWN TRAINING

DR. DAVID BRODY, medical director of the Marine Corps Marathon and a leading sports medic in Washington, D.C., has an answer for runners who ask, "What can I do to keep from falling apart when I can't run?"

He says to run exactly what you've been doing all along; just do it in deep water, wearing a water-ski vest, to protect the injury.

This isn't vague, untested advice. Dr. Brody studied eight runners for the training benefits of water-running. They volunteered to stop running on land for eight weeks and to substitute "runs" of equal to pre-marathon duration and intensity in the deep end of a pool.

They finished the test by running the Marine Corps Marathon. All of them improved their marathon times and suffered no foot-leg problems after two months off their feet.

Dr. Brody warns, however, that these athletes were marathon-trained before the study began. Someone with little or no such background probably couldn't expect to *get* into shape with this substitute activity. It is a way of *staying* fit.

High-school runner Mike McCollum had bad luck with foot injuries. Twice in one year, he hurt himself during racing seasons. He lost three weeks of track in his junior year and three more weeks of cross-country as a senior.

McCollum and his coach, Dwayne "Peanut" Harms, came up with a way to keep Mike fit while his feet were healing. He trained in a swimming pool, but not by swimming. He "ran" there.

Harms says, "Many doctors and coaches recommend the

pool during times of injury, but give little instruction on what to do there. Some athletes swim to maintain aerobic fitness. But I feel there are better ways for a runner to use the water.

"Before working with McCollum, I sent injured runners to the pool to run in the shallow end. They would take workouts of the usual types (distance, fartlek, intervals, etc.), duration (measured by time), and intensity (monitored by heart rate). The buoyancy of the water almost eliminated pounding, which would have aggravated the injury.

"Pool running worked fine for most problems—particularly muscle pulls and tendinitis. However, this kind of running didn't help two injuries: stress fractures of the feet and inflammations of the plantar fascia. Almost any degree of pushoff, on land or in water, irritated these areas."

After his first injury, a severe heel bruise, McCollum began training in the deep end of the pool while wearing a life jacket. Harms applied the same principles of training used on the track, allowing for distance days, speed days and interval days.

"For example, Mike would warm up by pedaling around the pool, imitating running form as closely as possible. Then he'd start a workout of, say, 10 times 72 seconds at three-fourths effort with 60-second rests between."

After three weeks of no dry-land running in the track season, McCollum improved his best two-mile time from 9:27 to 9:24, then dropped to 9:13 a week later.

He stress-fractured a foot during cross-country season. Doctor's suggestion: no running for three weeks. Coach's suggestion: pool training for three weeks. It worked again. Mike earned high-school All-American honors.

Coach Harms says, "I'm sure he came back so well partly because he is a fierce competitor. But he couldn't have competed at such a high level without being in top shape. His pool training kept him that way when he wasn't able to pound the ground."

Natural Reactions

Doctors don't necessarily make good patients, especially when they're trying to treat themselves. Dr. Victor Altshul is a psychiatrist, a professor in the Yale University School of Medicine. He also runs marathons, or did until a two-year siege of sciatica halted him.

"My injury was psychologically induced," he says. "I suffer from the classical Greek sin of *hubris*, which, loosely translated, means I always get too big for my britches."

In his case, this meant trying to run a sub-three-hour marathon, "a goal to which few people can less legitimately aspire." The hard training and racing hurt him, but also let him identify psychological stages he passed through while recovering:

1. "A *stage of denial*. For about a month, I simply denied I was hurt."
2. "A *stage of rage*. I became furious with my body for betraying me and expressed my anger by subjecting it to more abuse."
3. "A *stage of depression*. I grieved over a double loss: the loss of the capacity to run smoothly and painlessly, and the loss of the concept of myself as someone able to run a three-hour marathon."
4. "A *stage of acceptance*. My self-concept became more realistically that of an injured runner."
5. "A *stage of renewed neurotic disequilibrium*. With the subsidence of the injury, I became aware of the renewed tension between the need to stay within the limits of my talent and the grandiose claims of neurotic ambition."

Recovery can never be total as long as that fifth stage is not resolved.

J

Journal of a Journey

PERSONAL RECORD-KEEPING

DIARIES SERVE THE same purpose as home movies. So much of what you do in running is invisible, gone behind you as soon as you pick up your feet, that you need this reminder of where you've been and what you did there.

Diaries store old memories where you can see and touch them. You can open the book, say to January 19th, 1969, and recreate that day from the set of numbers on the page. You don't need many facts to trigger memories. The only two essentials are how far you ran and how long it took.

Any number of publishers are eager to have you put your numbers into their prepared diaries, but you don't really need anything that fancy for reporting facts. A calendar with a block of white space for each day will give you a month's worth of running on one page. So will a sheet of lined notebook paper.

Runners, of course, tend to be compulsive by nature. This

trait carries over from running to reporting on it. Neither place are you likely to settle for bare minimums. As the running habit escalates from one to two to four to eight miles a day, so does the number of lines spent telling about it. What had been trivia becomes critical detail.

Anyone who would swim 2½ miles in the ocean, bicycle 112 miles, and then run a marathon has to be somewhat compulsive. Entrants in the Ironman Triathlon in Hawaii do all three events back to back. *Sports Illustrated* has featured them.

Barry McDermott wrote, "Most of the Ironman contestants keep precise training diaries. To them, they are cancelled checks to peruse fondly. (Gordon) Haller (a former winner) logs not only every shred of physical activity, but also each morsel of food and the time it was consumed. Junk food is underlined. He records his pulse rate, his sleep time, injuries, and the quality of his day."

Tom Warren won the 1979 Triathlon. He "not only chronicles his daily exercise but makes copies that he sends each month to friends around the country."

Fanatics. That description leaped to mind when an old diary-keeper read this article. The second thing he thought was that he had been one of them once—not an Ironman but a keeper of similar training esoterica.

Each page of the diary designed by Fred Wilt told the day's story in dozens of items, listing everything the runner put into himself and everything that came out. If you wanted to know what he ate for lunch on November 22nd, 1960, he could tell you.

Years of putting checks and numbers onto these pages taught him what was important to his running and what didn't matter very much. Eventually he used so few of the boxes and wrote so many extra comments that he switched to blank paper. He finally reduced the essential facts to a line on a typical day and two to three lines for a race.

He suggests that you do the same. Keep the diary simple,

and you're more likely to keep filling it in. Don't let it drown in trivia. Decide which facts are important to you from this list:

1. When? (date and time of day)
2. Where? (location, name of course)
3. How far? (distance)
4. How fast? (running time)
5. Pace (per mile; list splits if it's a race)
6. Place (in race)
7. Quality (grade it A, B, C, D, or F; more on this later)
8. Weather (if it's a factor in the run)
9. Weight (taken under constant conditions)
10. Comments (unusual experiences)

Any or all of these facts add to a pool of raw material you can draw on later as you analyze data or make up stories about running. But even if you take the information no further, you can rerun these home movies of your life any time.

Days of running leave behind only individual footprints in a diary. You can't take much direction from them. But weeks, months, and years of running line up in a trail that points two ways. It shows where you have been before and where you might go from here.

The trick in turning your history into a better future is learning to read that trail. Where on it did you move easily and quickly? What wrong turns did you take? Where were its potholes that tripped you up? You smooth the path ahead by first looking back and processing the raw data that went into your book a day at a time.

Most runners already do two elementary kinds of analysis: listing personal records and keeping weekly mileage totals. The first gives historical and comparative value to times. The second begins to look at running as a set of connected steps, a long-term process.

Both lists are useful in their simplest forms—best times only for standard racing distances; miles added up once a week with no other training factors considered. But both types of information can do much more.

RECORDS ARE MEANT to be broken. They quit meaning anything if you don't have regular chances to break them, either because you seldom run a distance or because you have hit the ceiling of your ability and backed down.

When old marks move out of reach, make up new ones. Choose your records from this list so you'll always be able to break something:

1. All standard racing distances in both yard-mile and metric events, in each of the four running settings: road, cross-country, outdoor track and indoor track.
2. Best times on each of your frequently raced courses.
3. Fastest runs at each age. This gives you a chance to start new record lists on each birthday.
4. Biggest training day, week, month, year, and the longest streak without a day off.
5. "Reverse records"—slowest race times, longest layoff, and so on.

TOTALS. The problems with weekly mileage totals are that a week isn't long enough and mileage alone doesn't tell enough. Runners react to running and recover from it slowly. To you, seven days is a very short time. If you measure your work by that period, the numbers may distort what you do.

For instance, you normally do your long weekend run on Sunday. But you're busy that day and take it on Saturday instead. This week's total, with its two 15-mile runs, looks terrific. Next week's will be puny without any long ones. Yet the training effects of both weeks are identical.

Another example: You race a hard 10 kilometers on Saturday. Ideally you would give yourself all of next week to recover. But you don't want to fall below your 50-mile-a-week training goal. So you overwork.

Monthly, rather than weekly, accounting takes care of both problems. Thirty-day periods are long enough to smooth out the energy spurts and slumps, race buildups and recoveries, and switched-workout highs and lows. A month's total gives a clearer look at what you do.

The picture clears even more when you toss other factors into the analysis:

1. *Daily average*. This makes more sense than a monthly total, because the smaller number is easier to grasp and the months are different lengths. Divide the total by the number of days, even if you don't run them all.
2. *Racing percentage*. How much of the month's running is all-out? You probably can't stand more than 10 percent month after month.
3. *Weight and weather* (temperature). Keep average figures for the readings that have a direct bearing on running performance.
4. *Notes*. Include significant records, routine-disturbing injuries or illnesses, and so on. On months when you make notes, look at the numbers for the reasons. They may not show up immediately, but will as monthly patterns of highs and lows repeat themselves.
5. *Grades*. This is a measure of quality.

Making the Grade

RUNNING ATTRACTS US and holds our interest for two opposite reasons: objectivity and subjectivity. The sport offers the truth of numbers; today's times and distances can be compared accurately with any other day's. And running lets us decide for ourselves what value we place on these numbers; the interpretations of success and failure are most personal.

Runners make a fetish of checking and recording quantities of distance and time. We quote weekly, monthly, and yearly totals. We remember race times down to the second.

But we're more vague when we try to recall how a run or race felt. What was its *quality*, meaning in this case how well did it meet expectations of what good effort should be? We don't know, because we haven't paid as much attention to subjective measurements as objective ones.

Most runners' diaries are half-empty, holding plenty of numbers, but not telling how successful the run was in the runner's mind. To get a better idea, grade each run or race for quality—as a schoolteacher would grade an exam:

> **A** = exceeded normal distance, pace, or both.
> **B** = ran as expected.
> **C** = struggled to hold normal levels.
> **D** = forced to cut back.
> **F** = did nothing.

If you want to know how much you ran, look at the numbers. If you want to know how *well* you ran, the letter grade tells you. It tells this on single days, but these grades give more accurate readings for longer periods.

Just as the physical effects of mileage accumulate over weeks, months, and years, so do the psychological effects of pleasing or frustrating runs. Figure the monthly quality rating as a school would calculate a grade-point average. Each "A" earns four points, "B" gives three, "C" two, "D" one, and "F" zero. Divide the total by the number of days.

A quality reading above 3.00 means things are going right; find out what they are, and copy them in the future. An average in the 2.00 to 2.99 range indicates that all is not well; make subtle changes in the routine. A grade below 2.00 warns of serious trouble; take emergency action immediately.

In Your Own Words

Brian Maxwell wasn't trained formally as a writer. He is the distance coach at the University of California in Berkeley and one of the leading marathoners in North America. Years ago, he began writing stories about his races. Some of these eventually found their way into print, but Maxwell published them without compromising his personal style. He would have written the same way if no one had wanted to see it.

Running has thousands of hidden Maxwells. Something about the activity, maybe the fact that we spend so much time looking inside our heads, inspires the storyteller in us. We all love to talk out our adventures, and many of us go the next step to writing them down in diaries.

We now know that running is too good to belong strictly to the fast people. Writing is the same. It is too satisfying to be the exclusive property of professional writers. You may not have their talent, but they can't tell your story for you, just as no sub-4:00 miler or 2:15 marathoner can run for you.

Beginning to write is as simple as starting to run. Anyone who walks can run; anyone who talks can write. But would-be writers face two mental barriers, the "I phobia" and the "perfection syndrome."

Don't be afraid to say "I" a half-dozen times per paragraph. The diary is your book, and modesty has no place in it. Here you exercise your ego, letting it run on at will. A writer who is free to talk about himself seldom is at a loss for words.

Writers only block up when they try to write too perfectly—when they put style before content, or when they feel the eyes of a critical audience looking over their shoulder. They work best by putting pen to paper and letting the stream of consciousness flow. Adding, revising, and cutting come later, if ever.

John Steinbeck taught this. He told writers, "Put it all in. Don't try to organize it. Put in all the details you can remember. You will find that in a very short time things will begin coming back to you that you thought you had forgotten . . . Don't think of literary form. The form will develop in the telling. Don't make the telling follow a form."

Write out your feelings to the diary. The numbers may be the brains of your diary, but the words are its heart.

K

Know Yourself

A VIEWER AND A DOER

ONLY A RUNNER VERY SECURE in his or her self-image can watch a big marathon without feeling diminished by the experience. We live in the Age of the Marathoner, and we're now moving into a new era in which merely surviving the long race is not enough. The idea is growing that a "real runner" must run that far, *fast*.

As a longtime runner yourself, you should know better, but you forget as you stand at the finish line of a major marathon. You share very mixed feelings with yourself. The fan in you is thrilled by what you see. You feel happy for these runners, many of them friends, for the distance and speed they squeeze from themselves. But the runner in you threatens to shrink to insignificance as you watch people finish 26.2 miles at a pace faster than you can now run a single mile. You can't help agreeing that these are the real runners, and you are someone much less.

This is when you need to ask yourself, "What, exactly, is a real runner?"

The real runner is a viewer as well as a doer. Your own running is very important to you. You take it quite personally and are extremely proud of your efforts, knowing no one else could run them for you. But self-interest doesn't blind you to the fact that lots of other people run farther and faster. You can be amused, entertained, educated, and inspired by them without feeling intimidated.

To be a real runner is both to have heroes and to be one. Rating highest on your scale are those who make the most from the least and those who persist. You think quite highly of people like Ron Daws, who probably started with less talent than any Olympian ever has. You admire Jack Foster, who runs 2:20 marathons in his 50s—and does it without letting the sport run him. You think the world of Doris Brown Heritage and Nina Kuscik, pioneers of women's running who keep putting much more back into the sport than they ever took out. Real runners look to these people with admiration and not with envy. You don't need to want what heroes have when you already are a hero who has so much yourself.

For similar reasons, you aren't afraid to read. Insecure runners don't like to read about faster ones, because it makes themselves feel small and meaningless. The reading makes the real runner's world a million times bigger. But you must read selectively. A real runner's guide to reading a running magazine: don't try to read everything; be selective. Skip the ads for non-running products and the ads for gimmick items of no practical value to you. Flip past any article that begins with the statement, "Running changed my life"—unless you want a sermon. Avoid articles on beginning running, because if you hadn't already begun you wouldn't be reading the magazine. Pass by anything having to do with alternative exercises and most of what is written about supplementary exercises; you want to run. Don't read about medical problems that you don't have. Don't waste time on a diet piece, because you'll read another next month that contradicts it. Boycott stories of Hollywood stars who used running to improve their appearance, Washington politicians who use it to brush up their image, or prominent businessmen who use it to increase their productivity. Real runners want to read about real running.

The real runner knows that this sport has a rich history. You know the names of people who stopped running before you started. You feel like a friend to runners across the country and around the world whom you have never seen and will never meet. You know, and take pleasure in knowing, that this sport is much bigger than you are and that the only way you can remain a true part of it is to keep running and reading.

You are known as a real runner by the trivia you carry. You can't remember your own phone number or your current bank balance, but you can tell who missed medals by one place in the 1972 and 1976 Olympic marathons. You know that the two famous Kelleys of Boston both spell their last names with two "E"'s. You know that Kathrine Switzer only puts one "E" in her first name. You know that the last American to hold a world marathon record before Alberto Salazar was Buddy Edelen, and that Edelen's real first name is Leonard. You know that the first woman to break three hours was Beth Bonner and the second, just moments later, was Nina Kuscsik (two "S"'s). To paraphrase Eugene McCarthy's observation on politicians, you are smart enough to know the game and dumb enough to think it is important.

You're even better acquainted with your own racing statistics. Humble as they may be, they are your own. You have earned them with your own sweat and will never forget a second of them. You can tell—if someone would only ask—exactly how long ago you ran your first race, where it was, the time of day, the weather conditions, the size and quality of the field. You can tell exactly how many times you have raced since then and exactly what your times were in each one. You can list from memory your 10 best races of all time and your 10 worst. The real runner records all of his numbers, even when they hurt.

A real runner runs for the sake of running. Good health and fitness are important to you. So is racing. But those are by-products of the real thing, which is your everyday run. You have run through injuries and illnesses, when medical wisdom tells you to stop. You have gone long spells without racing, just to prove to yourself that you don't need this excitement as a motivator. You know the physical benefits of running, but would keep it up even if a government agency suddenly decreed "Running is hazardous to your health." You know the values of racing and know that road runs are here to stay, but would keep running if public officials suddenly decided that these races were a public nuisance and banned them.

You don't qualify as a real runner until you earn your battle scars—physical, psychic, or both. You don't truly know what running means to you until you have lost it for a while through injury or burnout. You come out on the other side of those problems knowing what is important, which is not necessarily being able to run fast but being able to run at all. Taking this thought further, you may not even become a real runner until your race times go into decline. Anyone can run when he's healthy and improving by leaps in each race. The real runner is one who still wants to run with nagging pain and still feels it's worth doing slowly. You know that not running would feel worse than putting up with chronic injury. You agree with world-record 5000-man Dave Moorcroft, who has said, "If I hadn't been a fairly good runner, I'd still enjoy being a fairly bad one." You run because you must.

Long-term goals define a real runner. If you're real, you

aren't so worried about what you run in this week's race as with being able to run again the day after. You run as if there will never be any finish line. You have settled into a pace which you can carry on indefinitely. You look at your running life as if it were a marathon and one year of it as if it were a mile. You won't do anything in one of those pieces which might threaten the whole.

A real runner lives running. That isn't to say you're obsessed with it or think of little else every waking moment or dream of it every night. It's just part of you and everything you do. Running is not something you must make yourself do each day, but what you do as naturally as eating and breathing. You make no sacrifices for your run. It isn't time taken out of the day but a normal part of it. You have fully metabolized running into your daily routine, making it a habit. You may run less than one hour in 24, but you're a runner all day long. You automatically sift all other obligations past this question: "What effect will this have on my running?" The answer affects when you go to bed at night and get up in the morning, what you eat and drink, how you socialize and with whom, even where you live and the kind of work you do.

You stood watching the marathon pass by that Sunday morning. Almost everyone who saw and recognized you asked, "Why aren't you out here?" The comment was innocent, but it implied that something was wrong with your running commitment if you didn't join them in the sport's biggest challenge.

The next morning, you returned to the same course. Rain was pouring down. A path usually so filled with runners that it almost needs a traffic cop was empty this day. As you ran alone, you wished you could shout back to yesterday's racers, "Why aren't you out here?"

You felt miserable as the water ran down the back of your jacket and the clammy pants stuck to your legs. But you would have felt more miserable if not running. That's a mark of a real runner.

PSYCHED OUT

"I FAILED," NED SACHS announces when the results of his test arrive in the mail. He had taken the Athletic Motivation Inventory offered by Drs. Bruce Ogilvie and Thomas Tutko at San Jose State University. The 200 or so multiple-choice questions measure 11 psychological traits judged to be important for athletic success.

Sample questions:

- "I like to be praised when I do well: (a) always (b) often (c) sometimes"
- "I enjoy getting into arguments about athletics: (a) often (b) sometimes (c) never"

A computer scores the test. It compares the subject with all others in the same sport and at the same level of competition. It ranks him on a percentile basis, meaning in running terms that a score of 80 in a particular trait is like placing 20th in a race with 100 runners. The computer printout gives a detailed analysis of the subject's thinking, and it assesses his chances of mentally cutting it in competition.

"I failed," Sachs says, "but I wasn't worried about failing. I worried that I might pass—that buried drives had been powering me through all my years of running, rather than a sincere attachment to running itself. I wondered if my whole view of running had been built on a lie—that running for fun was an elaborate rationalization without any basis in fact."

The comparative percentages told him quite clearly that he was subnormal among runners—a running retard, so to speak. He scored significantly below 50 percent in all but two of the 11 measured traits. Eight were in the bottom third. And in two areas, he ranked in the lowest 10 percent.

The printout told Ned, "This athlete was candid in acknowledging his undesirable attitudes. He did not attempt to make himself look good in answering the test questions and may have presented a negative image of himself."

Attitudes "undesirable" to whom? Sachs wants to know. "Negative image" by what standard? But the computer wasn't programmed to answer. It simply listed scores and comments, starting from the bottom:

1. Coachability (5 percent)—"Seems to have lost complete respect for coaches. This attitude is reflected in his extreme independence to the point of being aloof."
2. Aggressiveness (10 percent)—"Extremely non-aggressive athlete who rarely asserts himself. Feels the aggressive elements of sports are unappealing and nonrewarding."
3. Self-Confidence (20 percent)—Extremely lacking in self-confidence and has no faith in his competence. Great deal of difficulty in handling new or unexpected situations."
4. Mental Toughness (20 percent)—"Very sensitive, tender-minded athlete who will rarely face reality in a direct, positive manner."
5. Leadership (20 percent)—"Would rather follow than lead and will refrain from assuming responsibility."
6. Guilt-Proneness (25 percent)—"Not inclined to take personal blame when things go wrong. Because he is slow to admit errors, it will take longer to modify his negative behavior."

These were Sachs' lowest six scores, all in the bottom quarter of the running population. He barely moved into the middle of the pack with his next four traits, though they did tend to brighten the earlier picture painted of him.

   7. Drive (35 percent)—"Will set only modest goals for himself. He is not really competitive and will not readily accept challenges."

   8. Conscientiousness (35 percent)—"Prone to break or bend rules which are contrary to his desires. Will interpret even just demands to be a denial of his individual freedom."

   9. Emotional Control (50 percent)—"For the most part is able to handle his feelings. However, when competitive stress runs unusually high, tension may interfere with his performance."

 10. Determination (60 percent)—"Will generally put in required amount of time, but probably will not devote much extra."

Only in the area of trust (85 percent) did Ned shine. The computer said he has an "above-average capacity to trust and accept others without questioning their intentions. Not inclined to be jealous."

"If I had to choose one of the 11 traits where I would like most to look good," Sachs says, "this last would be it. But what do I believe? Am I 'extremely aloof and uncooperative' (see 'coachability,' the lowest score), or 'highly open and tolerant' (see 'trust,' the highest)?

"Aside from this apparent contradiction, the conclusions sit well with me. I'm happy to see that I don't have some of the least admirable traits of athletes—that I apparently haven't surrendered (1) control over my own recreation, (2) respect for fellow runners, or (3) human proneness to feel and to fail. I'm not at all sad to see that I don't possess unquestioning obedience, a killer competitive instinct, or dedication and drive to the point of obsession."

The computer printout ended by saying, "Please remember that this test was designed specifically for athletics and may not be applicable to other areas."

Sachs says, "I doubt that personality traits can be turned on and off quite that easily. Overly competitive behavior isn't likely to stop at the locker room door, and it may not look so impressive in civilian clothes."

Then he adds, "But this is for the psychologists to decide. They've satisfied me that there is indeed a run-for-fun personality and that I have it. I don't need the traditional success orientation to keep me going. In fact, for my purposes, I'm probably better off without it."

L

Little Lies

WHENEVER TWO OR more runners gather, each has a friend. Runners speak an international language of times and distances, victories and injuries. So in this most universal of sports, a runner never needs to feel lonely.

There is a flipside to this togetherness, though. Whenever two or more runners gather, they swap lies so freely that they put fishermen to shame. No runner is so secure that he doesn't occasionally retouch the truth to make himself look better.

The bars are full of ex-milers who once ran "down around 4:20." Someday these bars will be just as crowded with "about 2:40" marathoners. The further we move away from a race, the faster it grows. The improvement factor is about one second per mile per year. A 4:39.9 mile in 1962 becomes just under 4:20 in '82. Today's 2:49:59 marathon will drop into the low 2:40s by the turn of the century.

So whenever you hear anyone telling times, ask, "What year was that?" and make an automatic conversion upward.

Likewise, never accept training mileages or paces as stated. A runner, not wanting to appear lazy in the company of other runners (who lie for the same reason), exaggerates his weekly distance as follows: adds up the mileage for the best seven days of the last month, then tacks on a few extra to be safe. Daily totals are even easier to inflate. Just take one of the better days and imply that it is an average, as in, "I run 10 miles a day."

If you want the truth, ask to see a runner's diary. Few runners intentionally lie to these pages.

Time and distance figures don't lie, but the people quoting them do. One young man we'll call Mike ran with another athlete one afternoon. They cruised along smoothly and comfortably at what looked like seven-minute mile pace.

Later, Mike boasted, "We took one hell of a 12-mile run. We started out at 5:15 pace, then cut it down to five. And we checked one of those miles at under 4:50."

Giving Mike considerable benefit of doubt, he might have mismeasured his course. Routes checked by car usually fall short by 100 yards a mile, about half a minute for each mile at 7:00 pace. Rough guesses miss by twice that much distance and time, always in the runner's favor.

Only a rookie would believe such false readings, and Mike is no rookie. He races often and well. He averages 5:15 for six miles. But since this was the *slowest* pace of his alleged training run at twice this distance, he must fib again by saying of his races, "I had an off day," or, "I only ran for a workout." The lying eventually catches up with the liar.

We may repeat our lies so often that we start believing them ourselves. And we hear so many lies told that we may doubt other runners even when they tell the truth.

If you set a personal record, you say, "I ran up to my potential."

If your friend sets one, you say, "You had an unusually good day."

If someone else sets one, you and your friend agree, "The course had to be short."

Such suspicions reach to the world-record setters. Derek Clayton raced his 2:08:34 marathon (which stood as a record for 12½ years) in the Dark Ages of the sport when course-measurement techniques were primitive.

Just before that mark fell, a writer questioned the course distance at length and concluded: "It appears that the only question remaining is not if the course was short, but by how much. Let's stop worshipping at the shrine of 2:08:34."

Clayton responded that he had warned officials of a possible world's fastest time in that race. He had urged the Belgians to be accurate, and they'd assured him that the course was measured by a wheel attached to a car. A recheck after the marathon had given a reading just six meters short of the full distance.

Runners being skeptics, we prefer to believe a reporter writing a dozen years after the fact rather than a runner who was there in 1969. If we can't run on Clayton's level, we try to drag him down to ours.

Meanwhile, we also try to pull ourselves up closer to the stars and away from the masses. We don't want to be lumped with LSDers and fun-runners, so we say we do hard, serious running, even as the facts state otherwise.

LSD means long, slow distance. While the letters are widely known, the concept behind them isn't. Part of the problem is the name. LSD implies going as long as you can, as slowly as you can, and adding up as much weekly mileage as you can.

On the contrary, this is a concept of moderation in distance and pace—neither too long nor too short, too slow nor too fast. That message got lost somewhere in the translation from theory to practice, however, and LSD has become linked in many minds with endless, half-hearted slogging.

Ambitious runners now echo Sebastian Coe's line: "The only thing long, slow distance does is make you a long, slow runner."

This can happen, but the fact remains that most runners take some LSD as originally defined: comfortable running at about a minute per mile slower than marathon race pace or two minutes below all-out mile speed.

Several mornings a week, Alberto Salazar runs on a wood-chip trail in Eugene, Oregon. He glides along at six-minute pace. This looks fast to someone who can't *race* this fast. It is tempting to conclude that Salazar pushes himself all the time, and this is what separates him from LSDers.

In fact, Salazar spends more time in the comfort zone—in other words, doing LSD-type mileage—than most of us, simply because he runs a lot more. Six-minute pace is comfortable for one who races in the four-to-five range. But on top of this, Alberto adds the harder speedwork that most of us avoid, and in general takes his sport much more seriously than we do.

Brian Christian hasn't trained seriously in 15 years. But he still remembers his old speedwork, since its legacy remains in his feet and legs as he limps out of bed each morning.

"In the 1960s, we trained on little else but speed," he says. "The meat-and-potatoes workout at my college was 20 quarters on the track, averaging 65 seconds each. Our occasional 'slow overdistance' run was four miles at 5:30 pace."

When Christian first went a mile or two past those four and a minute or two above 5:30 pace, his running friends asked, "Why are you running so far and so slowly?" He still does the same type of running, but his old friends now ask, "Why do you do so little and run it so fast?" Brian hasn't changed his LSD routine, but the definition of LSD has changed.

He says, "Remembering—as I do when I step out of bed each day—what true speedwork is, I laugh out loud whenever anyone accuses me of training fast. I chuckle to myself when I hear a runner say, 'None of that LSD stuff for me. I only do high-quality work.' I'm sure his diary would show that he seldom trains within a minute per mile of race pace."

That training only seems fast now because so many people run so much slower. Only the Salazars, the elite of the sport, ever do work of the 20-times-440 variety which everyone once suffered through. Fortunately, only the most serious athletes now risk that kind of quality work, which still produces more victims than survivors.

Few of us ever get serious enough to meet these standards on the road or track, but we can carry our illusions into conversation by giving ourselves impressive titles and rejecting others.

The worst name anyone can call us is "jogger." Bernard L. Gladieux, Jr., of the American Running and Fitness Association writes that the word "jog" and its derivatives have fallen into disfavor, so much so that his organization has changed its name from National Jogging Association.

"The term 'jog' seems to many to connote an activity somehow not worthy of the serious athlete," Gladieux says. "It is, some think, an activity people enter into before they are capable or fit enough to run."

He tells of a young boy who mislabeled one of us. The offended athlete shouted back, "I'm a *runner*, a *runner*, a *runner!* Get it straight next time, kid."

The boy's response: "Then how come you're jogging?"

One of the big plusses of distance running is also one of its greatest problems: The elite mix freely with the average. It's as if the duffer in golf got to tag along with the professional tour, or the sandlot baseball player got to bat in the National League.

We have to remind ourselves from time to time that, no matter how impressively we talk, most of us are still duffers and sandlotters. Lying to each other about how good we are is harmless enough—so long as we remember that talking like a big-leaguer doesn't make us one.

LYING DOWN

A QUICK WAY TO TELL a new runner from an old one is to ask about his accomplishments. The novice probably will embellish his, while the veteran will more likely play his down.

Jim Fixx, the *Complete Book* writer, tells about the second type of liar. His neighbor, at age 50, still runs marathons in 2:40.

"He once told me," says Fixx, "he trained only seven miles a day."

Fixx asked him to explain how he got such good times on so little running. The neighbor said, "Good genes, I guess."

"One night at about midnight," Fixx recalls, "I flew in from Paris. Jet-lagged and unable to sleep, I decided to relax myself by going for a short run. On a dark road, I saw a running figure in a sweatsuit coming toward me. As it got closer, I realized it was my neighbor."

Fixx asked, "What in the world are you doing at this hour?"

"Ten miles," the man said.

"But I thought you told me you ran only seven miles a day."

"That's true. Seven miles a day—and 10 miles at night."

No veteran has run better, longer than Jack Foster. The New Zealander didn't start running until he reached his early 30s. It wasn't until almost 10 years later that he ran his fastest marathon. He averaged five-minute miles in that one. Now past age 50, he still runs 2:20 for that distance.

Yet to hear Foster describe his running, you would think he was little more than a neighborhood jogger. He says he doesn't train. Oh, he runs—though only about half as much as the youngsters who race no faster than Jack does. Seventy miles is a good Foster week. He runs once a day and takes frequent days off.

What Foster doesn't say is that few of those miles pass slower than six-minute pace, or that he runs over steep sheep-grazing hills, or that he takes hard bike rides on his "days off." He does the work. He just doesn't choose to think of it as training.

To Jack, "train" means to get ready for the future. It implies that the only value to a run is what it might return later in a race.

He says, "I run for today and let tomorrow take care of itself. I would run the same way even if I never raced."

That is truth, spoken as only a mature and secure runner can speak it.

M

Mistakes and Myths

Cunning Running

Don Kardong, an Olympic marathoner, once said that running is no more complex than putting one foot in front of the other . . . "and as long as you remember to alternate feet, you can't run into too much trouble."

That isn't quite true. Agreed, running is simple. But modern life isn't. It has been so long since some people ran that they no more remember how to do it right than they know how to trap and skin a rabbit for dinner.

Despite all of the articles and books written to keep runners from making mistakes, we see the old ones repeated so often that we have to restrain ourselves from grabbing people by the T-shirts and saying, "No, no! That isn't how it's done. Try this."

Don't risk offending an ex-fullback or frightening a housewife with your zeal. If you know someone who fits any of the descriptions below, leave this book open to the appropriate

89

page at the breakfast table. It might make better reading than the back of a cereal box.

SUNNY-DAY RUNNER. New runners believe the weathermen who report from their air-conditioned, fluorescent-lit studios, "It's a gorgeous day today," when the sun shines warmly, or "another miserable day" when a cool, gray mist descends. The roads and tracks fill up on the sunny days and lie empty —except for the grizzled veterans—on the latter type. We old folks know that the best running days come when the sun is hiding and the temperature is too chilly for anything except moving briskly. If we feel warm enough when we start, we know we'll soon feel too hot.

Tip: Save the longest and hardest runs for the coolest, darkest, dampest days or times of day. Only mad dogs and masochists go out in the noonday sun.

RUN-IN-PLACE RUNNER. This one thinks running isn't official or real unless it goes around (and around and around) a track. He circles it like a merry-go-round horse. Worse, he may drive miles to get to the track and fight for the parking space nearest the gate. He spends more time getting there, parking and locking the car, and driving home again than he does running.

Tip: Save the track for what it was meant to be—a place to race and then only for a few laps. Save the car for what it was intended to do—take long trips and haul loads. Run closer to home and in more natural settings.

OVERDRESSED-UNDERSHOD RUNNER. He dresses more for looks than comfort. The $80 jogging suit (can't say sweats anymore!) that felt comfortable for standing around becomes too warm within a mile, and parts of it are tied uselessly around the waist. The $15 imitation running shoes that looked like the real thing and felt okay in the store cause increasing misery.

Tip: Save the fancy clothes for non-running wear. Better yet, spend the money saved from clothing to invest in the best possible shoes.

MAKE-EVERY-SECOND-COUNT RUNNER. He is hard-driving, competitive in everything he does—an ex-athlete who still thinks like one. He put off starting to run for years because, "I don't have time." He still misses several days a week because he won't make time. When he does run, he allows exactly 15 minutes for it. He stretches twice, times himself for a mile on the track or the same measured route each day, swears to himself if he doesn't break his record, then rushes away before he stops gasping.

Tip: Rushing gives nothing but numbers on a watch. Rushing strains the heart-lung system, as well as almost everything else; relaxed running trains them. Rushing aggravates "hurry sickness"; relaxing relieves it. Allow time to go distances that can't be rushed.

CAREFUL-NOT-TO-BREAK RUNNER. He had never been an athlete before starting to run. He tiptoes into his runs as if they were going to attack him. He runs on little six-inch strides, so slowly and quietly that no one can hear him. He looks around self-consciously and freezes if anyone looks back. He stops when he breaks a sweat.

Tip: Everyone has a just-right pace that is neither too fast *nor too slow*. Too fast is a painful struggle. Too slow is clumsy and inefficient. Go fast enough to feel like a runner, not someone a fast walker could pass.

A-LITTLE-GOES-A-LONG-WAY RUNNER. He thinks if a few laps around the track feel bad, more can only make it worse. He never finds out that running effort doesn't progress logically. To a point, longer is easier. No one feels very good in the early running, which is a time for warming up. Runners who never go beyond 15 to 20 minutes never feel running at its smoothest and best.

Tip: Work through those first minutes to get into the part that makes running worth doing.

BIG-FOOT RUNNER. He slams down hard on the heels and then slaps with the forefoot. You can hear him coming before you see him. Shoemakers love him for the speed with which he wears out their product, doctors for the pounding he gives his legs and back.

Tip: Run from the hips down, not the feet up. Lift with the strong muscles of the buttocks and upper legs. Spring with the ankles. Use the feet as rolling shock-absorbers. This produces the quietest running, which is also the best running.

WHAT-DO-I-DO-WITH-MY-ARMS RUNNER. He runs like a soldier at attention—arms straight and stiff at his sides—or with his arms high and tight, like a boxer trying to protect his face from an attacker. Either way, this runner would be better off removing the arms and leaving them home. They just get in the way of running.

Tip: The arms aren't just along for the ride. They counterbalance what's happening below. Use them. Swing them with a relaxed drive, keeping the elbows at about a 90-degree angle and unlocked.

RUN-TO-BE-SEEN RUNNER. A mile is a mile anywhere. The body doesn't know the difference between a mile on Main Street and one run on a country road. But the head knows that running and cars and crowds don't mix well. Drivers and walkers know it, too. The sight of a runner often brings out the worst in them. Many of them would like to get rid of runners. They may assault you with weapons ranging from words to bottles to laws to guided one-ton missiles traveling at 55 miles an hour.

Tip: Hide! Run away from people, not among them. They don't want to see runners, and the runner may not care to see the reactions he brings out of them.

RIGHT-IS-WRONG RUNNER. He thinks he is a driver, subject to the same laws and protected by the same armor. He takes a wide path on the right side of the road and takes the right-of-way without looking to see who else claims it. He worries about arcane injuries and ignores the threat of death that passes within inches of him every few seconds.

Tip: The right side of the road is the wrong side for a runner. Stay on the left to see better what might hit. Right-of-way is a legal concept, not a practical one. Run defensively, being aware of every driver on the road.

LONG-RUNNING MYTHS

YEARS AGO, when a young writer published his first articles, readers controlled how he felt about his work. Positive letters made him think his Pulitzer would come any day. Negative ones made him wonder why he had wasted paper for his words.

Seeing these manic-depressive tendencies, an old editor said, "Kid, you have to realize that people don't mean everything they write. Praise sounds stronger than they intend it, and so does criticism. If you want the truth, automatically cut the best and worst of the comments in half."

That advice applies now to what is being said by both friends and enemies of running: those who run and think anyone who doesn't is a physical retard, and those who don't and think any runner is nuts. Both types shout their positions too loudly.

The praisers seem to say:

> • Once you get into shape, it's easier and more fun to run than to drive a car . . . except when you race. Then you risk running into "the wall," which feels like being hit by a car.
> • Running makes you immune to the diseases and failures of modern man. Your only worry is being shot by a jealous husband at 85.

• This is a drugless "high." After a half-hour of
running at a "meditative" pace, you float away
into euphoria and don't come down for hours.
• Running is a religion with its own gospels,
saints, rituals, and places of worship. The obli-
gation of all true believers is to carry The Word
to pagans who don't yet believe.

The critics answer this oversell with essays like Frank Deford's in *Sports Illustrated.* "I am sick of joggers, and I am
sick of runners," Deford writes. "I don't care if all the people
in the U.S. are running or are planning to run or wish they
could run. All I ask is, don't write articles about running and
ask me to read them.

"I don't ever again want to read about the joy of running,
the beauty, the ecstasy, the pain, the anguish, the agony, the
rapture, the enchantment, the thrill, the majesty, the love,
the coming-togetherness, the where-it's-at-ness. I don't ever
again want to hear running compared to religion, sex, or ultimate truth."

The truth about running rests about halfway between
quasi-religious praise and don't-cram-it-down-my-throat criticism. Perhaps runners can view their sport more realistically
and non-runners can look at the activity more tolerantly if
we expose some half-truths:

1. *The fun.* Running isn't fun all the time, and it never is
   fun for very long. Parts of each day's run—and often
   whole runs—are no fun at all. You work through the bad
   spells because a couple of miles a day, or a day or two a
   week are satisfying. These moments make up for the
   trouble of finding them.
2. *The ease.* Running isn't easy for anyone past puberty,
   and the kind of running we do (long, steady, and often
   on hard surfaces) isn't natural even for children. We
   adapt as all other athletes do—by learning a specialized
   skill that isn't much like the running we did on the
   playground as kids. We need specific instruction in how
   to run this odd way.

3. *The pain.* Runners face different types and degrees of pain. Good pains warn us away from trouble before we hurt ourselves too much. Bad pains come when we ignore the good and can't run as a result. Blisters, sore muscles, labored breathing, and temporary fatigue are not reasons to run or to stop running, but only byproducts of running. "The wall" that runners talk about is nothing more mystical than a warning against training too little or starting too fast.

4. *The health.* Be slow to cite medical evidence either about the miracles that running works on the body or the damage it causes. No other sport, from football to skiing, is praised or condemned as much for its physical results. Doing so makes running seem more a form of therapy or torture than a sport like the others.

5. *The high.* Think of running not as a natural high but as a natural laxative. It throws off the wastes stuck in the body and mind. This cleansing usually takes about a half-hour. After that, the way is clear for smooth running and good thinking. Instead of thinking this is a mystical experience, consider it as the way we're supposed to feel when not constipated.

6. *The religion.* Both religion and running involve making sacrifices now for greater joy later. But this is as far as they go together. In fact, the two are more opposite than alike. Religion implies belief in a force bigger and better than any person can be. Running is indulgence of that self and what it can become. There's nothing wrong with a little self-worship, as long as it goes by its real name.

We runners need to praise running only for what it is: a sporting event. There are safer ways to exercise than this, better ways to meditate, quicker ways to get high, truer ways to find religion, easier ways to have fun.

Running gives some of these things, of course. But praising them too highly hides what runners really have here: a sport which like all sports has both pain and joy, risk and reward.

N

Nothing to Lose

No Losers, No Pain, No End

ONLY ONE WINNER? Any runner who has ever been part of an organized athletic team has been force-fed the idea that second place means nothing; defeat is a kind of death; only the winner is allowed to be happy. This may sound noble on paper. But what it means in reality is that a sport can produce only one winner standing above a mob of losers. Even that winner doesn't get to stand there very long before someone from the mob rises up to knock him from his peak.

Because the peak is so small and the slopes below are so crowded, most climbers get trampled on the way up, and the athlete at the top spends less time enjoying the view than worrying about falling off.

A dramatic example of this mountain-climbing is Jim Ryun. He raced right to the top as a boy. At 17, he was at Olympian heights; at 19, a world mile record-holder; at 21, psyched out so badly that he quit running.

Ryun violated the Satchel Paige Law. As long as the miler looked ahead to higher and higher peaks, he couldn't lose. He ran strongly, smoothly, confidently, without seeming to take much notice of who ran against him.

Then he reached the top, stopped, and looked at the hungry pack at his heels. He did what Paige said an athlete should never do: looked back and saw that others were gaining on him.

This frightened Ryun. He started running less to win and more to keep from losing. He lost first his confidence, then his races—once falling to a 4:21 mile, several times dropping out to avoid the humiliation of finishing far back.

Jim hoisted himself back up to a pretty high level. He deserves credit for that. But he never got to the peak that the Ryun of old had climbed. So many observers rated his career as a failure that Ryun himself began believing it.

PAIN EQUALS GAIN? Most runners grew up with that cliché, too. As athletes, we were taught that comfortable running was only a warm-up. The real building began when a workout started to hurt. The more a run hurt, the more good it did—the farther it pushed back the "pain barrier."

Derek Clayton served as a role model. He trained hard, perhaps harder than any marathoner ever has. Maybe that's why he set a marathon record that lasted 12½ years.

When training to a peak, Clayton ran up to 200 miles a week. He didn't just pitter-pat through those miles, either. He believed there was no sense in running much slower in practice than he did in a race. So his base pace in training was five minutes a mile.

A typical weekend run for Derek was a full marathon in 2:20 to 2:25. Not content with doing just that in the morning, he would return in the afternoon for another 10 miles at five minutes each.

The reward for this routine was his world record. The immediate price was chronic fatigue. (Clayton once ran himself into such a state that he smacked into a tree while training.) The long-term price was chronic injuries. (During his career, Derek suffered through nine surgical operations: from back to knee to Achilles tendon.)

Enduring all of this pain, day after week after month, simply wore down his soft tissues. Clayton reached some of the highest peaks in the sport, but he also endured some of its deepest valleys.

More than anything else, Clayton was a competitor. The goal that means most to a competitor is not a record. That only indicates he has beaten a time and a mechanical object, the watch. He wants an Olympic gold medal, which shows he has beaten all fellow competitors.

Clayton never won an Olympic medal. He was injured during the Mexico City Games, which he entered with the fastest time. He was injured again at Munich, when he also was the fastest runner in the field. He retired before Montreal, feeling somewhat bitter about his "failures."

HANGING IT UP? There can be no life as a runner once fast racing ends? The continuing stories of Jim Ryun and Derek Clayton say otherwise.

When Ryun turned pro after the 1972 Olympics, he said, "I've never gotten anything from my running. It's time I finally started earning something for all this work."

That was a typically enigmatic Ryun statement. It could have meant that he'd never earned any money before, but that probably wasn't true; payoffs to "amateurs" in track go back to the 1960s and before.

Ryun probably meant that because he had never reached his most important goal—Olympic gold—he had achieved nothing. If he couldn't be a famous Olympic champion, he'd settle for being a rich pro miler instead.

The pro circuit never really got going. It folded after a couple of dull years, leaving Ryun without riches and with dwindling fame.

But he isn't bitter now. He runs five or six miles a day and likes it as he never did when he chased records and medals. He still races—not a mile on the track but longer distances on the road.

Ryun says, "People beat me. But that doesn't trouble me, because I know that's a thrill for them. I've always felt that a person shouldn't be frustrated as an athlete or in life if they're giving their best and maybe don't come out on top."

Ryun has finally come out on top. With a view like he has now, he's as much or more of a winner than he was when he ran a mile in 3:51.

The same can be said for Derek Clayton. When he retired after the 1972 Olympics, he made a blunt and bitter statement. He said, "I can honestly admit now that I've never enjoyed a single minute of my running, and I'm relieved to be finished with it."

His career apparently had ended like too many others. At the last finish line, all of that pain hadn't equaled gain. It had added up only to more and more pain, until finally it had eroded his health and enthusiasm to the point where he saw no reason to push on.

Clayton stopped—but not for good. After a few months away from running, he started missing it. He didn't miss the 200-mile weeks and the marathons that had beaten him up so badly. He missed something about the daily routine of running itself.

Derek began to run again. He limited himself to a quick five miles or so a day. Years later, he still does the same thing. He said in a recent talk that running has changed for him: from being grinding work that he barely tolerated to being "one of the bright spots in my day."

The running that Clayton does now is an answer to all three of the Great Lies of the sport. He runs without pain, but who is to say he isn't gaining? He wins no races of note, but who is to say he isn't a winner? His serious racing ended a decade ago, but he is moving proof that running life goes on after the best races have been run—and that this new life can be just as rich as the old in its own quieter way.

BIG SPORT, HIGH SPORT, TRUE SPORT

THE OLYMPICS ALMOST ENDED FOREVER in Munich, 1972, because they had taken on too much importance as a political staging area. Bil Gilbert, who coached a girls' track team besides writing for *Sports Illustrated,* wrote a brilliant piece for the magazine then. He talked about his version of the three levels of sport:

"There is first True Sport, the manifestation of man's seemingly innate urge to play. True Sport is organized for and often by participants, and is essentially a private matter like eating or making love."

In our terms, True Sport is everyday running—not training with a goal in mind, but simply running for its own sake.

"High Sport is True Sport raised to the level of art by the talent, even genius, of its participants. It is public in the sense that all art is public. Great music, painting, literature, or sport is incomplete until that time when it is displayed, judged and acclaimed."

High Sport is racing and training for races, working toward one's own definition of perfection.

"Finally, there is Big Sport in which elements of True Sport and High Sport are present, but are modified by other considerations—notably commerce and politics."

Big Sport is the Olympics and other quasi-professional meets where athletes of Olympic ability gather.

True Sport is the play of children or of people who for a moment want to be like children again. There is no special preparation needed for play. Graduating to High Sport means putting an element of training into it.

"High Sport," Gilbert said, "is the creation of geniuses,

the exceptionally talented and passionate. It satisfies the same needs as other arts. It provides a medium and a method of expression by which the talented can comment on themselves and their world. High-Sport artists also serve their audiences by stimulating them to consider the nature of man and the world."

In Gilbert's words, True Sport is to High Sport as a craft is to an art, and Big Sport is to the other two as a "plastic angel is to sculpture and pottery."

He didn't see much of a future for Big Sport. "Given the tenacity with which all institutions seek to preserve themselves," he said, "and the considerable resources of many of our institutions, [the professional and pseudo-amateur circuits] may linger for some time. As they struggle to maintain themselves, it seems probable that they will be decreasingly concerned with sport and become increasingly show-biz operations."

Gilbert seemed to welcome the predicted decline and fall of show-biz sports. He saw no serious consequences of it, "since even now they serve little purpose other than perpetuating themselves."

As for the future of True Sport (and, by implication, High Sport), Bil Gilbert said it "seems to be in as good or better shape than ever. Because True Sport is necessary and useful, it would appear to have about the same survival prospects as those of man himself."

O

Opportunities for Change

CALIFORNIA FAULT LINES

BILL RODGERS FLEW into Southern California from the Boston winter.

"After getting off the plane," he told a reporter, "I ran in a light drizzle. There weren't more than six people in the park, and they were jogging. In Boston, there would have been many more people—running."

He described a run at home that week in 25-degree weather, chilled down below zero by a strong wind.

"We all went out and ran," Rodgers said. "I think the adversity of training in Boston or New York makes you tougher, mentally and physically. Having to cope with the real bad weather toughens you up. I think it's a definite advantage for us in the East to face the adversity all the time. I wonder if people here (in California) would face that."

Rodgers isn't the first runner to make that comment. Jim Ryun, the best miler of his era, once was asked if he envied

Californians as he slogged through a foot of Kansas snow, bundled in three layers of clothes to keep out the cold.

Ryun said he'd be a fool to claim that he liked these conditions or the sticky 100-degree heat he faced on the other side of each year. But he thought that enduring the elements the way he did made him tougher than runners in California. When race conditions weren't perfect, and when the pace began to grind on all runners equally, he felt that his training gave him an edge.

California, the largest state with the most runners, enjoys no statistical edge over the others as a producer of top racers. The 1980 Olympic Trials showed that. Men and women raced in eight events, 1500 meters through marathon. Twenty-four positions on the honorary Olympic team were filled. Of those who made it, only Julie Brown lived and trained in California.

California is thought to be long-distance heaven. Yet its first resident-runner finished only ninth in the Marathon Trial. And Frank Richardson wasn't truly a Californian. He'd just migrated there from Iowa for winter training. Iowans might argue that Richardson would have done better if he had stayed at home. In fact, he did improve his time by a few seconds after returning to the Midwest.

These statistics might prove the softness which Rodgers and Ryun attributed to Californians. However, an Eastern expatriate now living in the Golden State offers a different explanation.

Mark Epstein says, "California runners' problem is having things too nice—but not in the way Elsewherians think it's a problem."

He gives a personal example: "I moved here in the winter, going from snow to summer-like conditions in a couple of days. Easterners were still waiting for their tracks to clear, while Californians were already well into their track season. That season lasted from December to August. It started again in December after a short break for cross-country. Road races went on year-round.

"I raced myself dry, because I no longer had the seasons to protect me. In the East, just when I started to wear out, a cold winter or hot summer came along to end serious racing and force the break I needed. The natural turn of the seasons held me to alternate three-month-up-and-down cycles. Californians don't have that advantage. So unless they're wise or lucky, they never peak at the right time."

The main trouble with California runners, Epstein thinks, isn't that they're lazy but that their benign climate tempts them to run themselves into that beautiful ground.

RUNNING INTO WINTER

JACK MCMAHON LOVES THE WINTER. He views it not as a period to be suffered through on the run, or as a time to be waited out indoors, or as a time to give up his sport in favor of one more suited to the season. He looks forward to winter running and enjoys its unique offerings.

This is an essay for those who think like McMahon. This is not one of those stories warning of the dangers of snow and cold; you'll find nothing here about frozen lungs. This is not an appeal to find another winter sport, though there is nothing wrong with, say, cross-country skiing. This is not a guide to winter clothing; anyone who walks outside in winter knows how to cover up.

This is in praise of winter, written for runners who won't or can't stop when the thermometer sinks below freezing and the snow begins to fall.

McMahon's first runs were done in Illinois, where it was thought that the only sane thing for an athlete to do between November and March was to stay in the gym, shooting baskets. He didn't leave the gym voluntarily; he had to be forced outside.

"The saddest—and luckiest—day of my young life came when the basketball coach gently told me there would be no place on his team for a slow, near-sighted guard," McMahon says. "Until that day, I had lived to play ball. Earlier that year, I had failed at football because that sport had no room for a timid 130-pound linebacker. Track was my last chance as an athlete."

Jack decided to get a jump on the track season by running all winter, starting indoors because he still believed the rumor that his lungs would turn to Popsicles if he breathed too much cold air.

"If it's okay with you," he said to the basketball coach, "I'll just run right here around the gym floor."

The coach caught a loose ball, passed it back across the floor, then said, "I suppose it's okay, as long as you don't get in anybody's way. Just don't run here during ball practice."

Practice ended after six o'clock, and McMahon couldn't wait that long to run. So he planned to squeeze in 10 hard minutes before the players took the court. The first day, he worked the tight turns like a Grand Prix driver. The next day, he limped into the gym on blistered feet and stiff ankles.

"What's wrong?" the coach asked. "Not in shape?"

"His words stung me," Jack remembers. "I forgot my soreness, went to the locker room, laced up my high-topped canvas shoes, tied my floppy gray sweatpants just below my chest and slipped into my hooded sweatshirt that hung to my thighs. Then I went outside to stay.

"Winter running made me the runner I am now. That was not determined by what happened on the mild, sunny days of spring and autumn; anyone can be a fair-weather runner. My attachment to the sport was tested and hardened on the so-called bad days when the crowds outside had disappeared."

The human body is an efficient furnace but a poor air-conditioner. It operates on the 20-Degree Rule, which states that the effective temperature automatically rises this much during a run. So a balmy 70-degree day soon feels like a miserable 90, while a chilly 30 degrees turns into a comfortable 50.

This is one reason why any longtime long-distance runner grows to prefer cool weather, even cold and wet weather, to the other extreme. He can warm up easily on cold days but can't cool down efficiently on hot ones.

No one remains ecstatic about the weather all winter. But when you examine the reasons for grumbling about it, discomfort places far down the list. The worst part of winter running is its inconvenience. The short days push runs into the darkness. Drifted snow forces you onto major roads, where you are blinded by headlights. You spend more time dressing and undressing. Your pace slows by as much as a minute a mile.

STAY FLEXIBLE. That's the best two-word advice on winter running. Accept what you can't change, and change what you can't accept. Accept that you can't run as far as usual on some days, or at all on a few. Change from morning or evening running to noontime, at least for the longer weekend sessions.

More often than not, you can run something, and anything is better than nothing. If you can walk outside in winter, you can run there. Hibernating is for bears, not for humans.

PEAK EXPERIENCES

SHAKESPEARE WROTE that "these high, wild hills and rough, uneven ways draw out the miles and make them wearisome."

Ted Castle recalls these lines, not for their literary merit but for their truth, each morning as he runs toward home.

"I live on top of what a mountain man or race director

would call a 'gentle rise,'" he says. "But to a not-quite-reformed flatlander like me, this is a mountain. It climbs 500 feet in the last half-mile of each run."

For his first 20 years, Castle had never seen—let alone run up—a grade like this. Then he moved west from the wheat-fields of Kansas to the foothills of the Rockies.

"Early on, I feared and hated those climbs which intruded on every run," Castle says. "I swore I would cut them down to size through force of will. But the mountains shrugged off my efforts. The harder I tried, the earlier a climb ended."

Then an old mountain goat of a runner took Ted in hand and taught him a few things about running vertically.

"The first thing you have to realize," he told Castle, "is that you never 'beat' a mountain. It shrinks for no one, so you have to adapt to its demands. Adapt as if you were riding a 10-speed bicycle uphill. You know you can't ride your bike in high gear all the way. You have to shift according to the terrain. The idea is not to maintain a constant speed but to hold a *constant effort*. Shift into a lower and more economical pace, the way a biker gears down."

The mountain man taught Castle two more lessons on climbing, these dealing more with outlook than technique:

> • "The longer the climb, the better the view from the top."
> • "You can climb to a peak, but you always have to come back down the other side."

"I immediately adopted the lesson on gearing down," says Ted, "and made relative peace with the foothills where I ran each day. But I didn't fully grasp the meaning of the moun-taineer's philosophy until I took my graduation exercise on Pike's Peak in 1975."

Before that race, Rick Trujillo, then the King of the Mountains, said, "The secret for me is that I try to maintain my equilibrium at all times. I try to keep my breathing normal. If I get tired, I slow down. Near the top, I may walk for 20 or 30 steps until I feel like running again. I don't try to keep an even pace. Some runners do, but this doesn't work for me. On the mountain, every step is different than every other."

Trujillo reinforced the advice of working *with* the hill, not against it. He worked with this one well enough that day to run up the 14,000-foot peak and back down in record time. Ted Castle's efforts were less ambitious but no less successful by his standards.

That course really climbed two mountains, not one. At the base, 9,000-foot Mt. Manitou blocked the view of Pike's Peak. The race started with three to four miles over the shoulder of Manitou. Then the trail crossed a meadow with a relatively gentle slope for several miles.

Pike's Peak was only half-climbed after 10 miles. The last three miles to the top took almost as long as the distance leading up to it. The trail surface alternated between loose gravel and boulders. The switchbacks above looked like lines gouged from a sheer face. Thirty-minute miles weren't uncommon at this elevation.

"Near the top," Castle recalls, "I met Dr. Joan Ullyot as she headed back down the mountain. She looked gray-faced and deeply concentrated as she raced toward a women's round-trip record."

At a pre-race clinic, Dr. Ullyot had said, "When you get to the top, turn right around and head back down. Don't stop. If you do, you may be wandering around in a daze up there and never want to leave."

Ted says, "I had no intention of following her advice. I had worked hard getting to the top, and I wanted to take some time to enjoy the view."

He walked to the highest point on the mountain, and only then stood and looked out and down. The scene was too vast for his dizzy head to comprehend just then. He sat down on a rock and stared out dumbly toward the prairies to the east.

"I felt little sense of triumph," he says. "I didn't have any urge to shout, 'There, I beat you!' The mountain can't be bothered with such petty challenges. It had offered me temporary visiting privileges, which I humbly accepted. The view was spectacular from up there. But I knew I couldn't stay on top very long, because the air was too rare."

All peaks are nice places to visit, but we can't live on them.

P

Pacing Perspective

MOTION SICKNESS

TWICE EACH DAY, Kent Dawson runs or walks his two dogs. Well, the truth is that the big Labrador drags him, and the little mongrel tries to do the same. They are impatient animals. No matter how fast Dawson goes, it's always two steps too slow for them. They are always that far away from where they want to be.

The dogs strain against their leashes. If Kent yanks them back, they pull all the harder to get away. Nothing they do can make him go fast enough to please them. All they do is tire themselves out with their straining, spoiling what could have been a pleasant outing if they had trotted along at their master's side with some slack in their ropes.

"I know how they feel," Dawson says. "By nature, I'm like them. I strain against an invisible leash. No matter how fast it lets me go, I want to go a little faster. If the leash yanks me back into line, I pull harder to break free. Of course, this is as futile for me as it is for the dogs. All it does is wear me down—and spoil what could have been a nice trip if I'd moved at the natural pace of the moment."

Running first attracted him, he claims, because it gave him the illusion he was breaking the leash and hurrying all he wanted. The rope seemed long, but he still reached its end eventually. Chronic fatigue and injury were the end results of the hurrying.

Dawson says, "What seems to be the most rushed thing I do, my running, has taught me the most about slowing down. I first made my peace with pace there. I've been slow to transfer those lessons to the rest of my day, but I'm learning. I'm trying to cure myself of the disease that is more of a national epidemic than heart attacks or lung cancer."

Dr. Meyer Friedman of San Francisco named it "hurry sickness." He is one of the country's best-known running haters. But he can be forgiven for that, because he knows only one side of the running story. All he knows is the damage it does to a few hearts. He doesn't understand what happens in many runners' heads.

We can forgive him for calling our sport a "wretched chore," because Dr. Friedman has taught us about the Type-A personality and the hurry sickness which is either its cause or result. He defines the Type-A person this way:

"First, he worries about the fact that he is dreadfully behind in doing all the things he should and could do. Or he frets at delays in being seated in restaurants, boarding airplanes, being held up in traffic, and having people 'come to the point.' Or he frantically strives to obtain things worth *having*—a lovely home, a better position, a college education for his children—at the expense of the things worth *being*— a lover of the arts, a reader of good literature, and a devotee of the wonders of nature and mankind . . ."

"I am not a true 'A'," says Kent Dawson. "I may have been once, but through the years—thanks largely to the running lessons—I've progressed up to about an A-minus. I want to keep moving toward B. The price of being an A is too high."

Meyer Friedman is a heart doctor, and of course he worries about the Type-A person from this standpoint. "We're dead certain," he has written, "that this personality is extraordinarily prone to coronary disease. What I am saying—and we have much data to support it—is that whenever a man struggles too incessantly to accomplish too many things in too little space of time (thus engendering a sense of time urgency), or whenever a man struggles too competitively with other individuals, this struggle markedly accentuates the course of coronary disease."

Heart disease doesn't scare Dawson very much. In his mid-30s, he has much bigger and more immediate health worries than that, such as damaging his legs permanently or getting run down by a truck. What bothers him about hurry sickness is "what it does to me *now*, and what it might have done to my running if I hadn't taken the cure."

Dr. Friedman has said that Type-A runners "allocate 15 to 30 minutes to it. They have a miserable tendency to run the same distance daily, with the intent of increasing their speed. This, of course, is another variant of the numbers poison."

Dawson was poisoned once, but his antidote consisted of longer time periods for his run and no concern with speed outside of his infrequent races. He says, "If I hadn't quit racing daily, I either wouldn't have held together long enough to be running now, or I wouldn't have wanted to try."

Friedman again: "I have repeatedly asked patients to bring me a list of events which they frequently recalled with real pleasure. Not one of these lists ever contained a reference to the acquisition of numbers—though it was precisely a too-frenzied acquisition of such numbers that led to their heart disease and their becoming my patients."

We could change a couple of Dr. Friedman's words and

say the same things about why runners become ex-runners.

"I'm still a latent speedaholic when I run," Kent Dawson admits. "I go on a binge every few weeks and race the clock. But the rest of the time, my running is medicine for hurry sickness and not a symptom of the disease. If I can control it there, I can do it the rest of the day by employing similar techniques."

He works to reduce the feeling of having too much to do in too little time. He does this in two ways:

> • *Time*—"As in running, I make friends with time. Instead of fighting the clock, I cooperate with it. I don't think, 'This job has to be finished by noon.' I say, 'I'll get whatever part of it I can comfortably finish out of the way by noon; the rest can wait.' The hours pass easiest when I fall into a gentle, steady pace."
>
> • *Intervals*—"As in running, the easiest way to climb over any mound of work is one step at a time, breaking up the imposing whole into manageable pieces. If I have the choice between doing a lot of work all at once and doing a little bit steadily, over a period of days or weeks, I'll always spread it out. The way to work is as a marathoner builds for a race—little by little, day by day. Nothing worthwhile can be built overnight."

A hundred years ago, people couldn't hurry their travel. Most of the world plodded along at five miles an hour or slower, on or behind a horse or on foot. The automobile changed that. It put speed in everyone's hands, giving us the chance to go 10 to 20 times faster than before. Having that chance meant taking it.

Something no one has explained is why speed limits are set at 55 m.p.h., while cars are made to go twice that fast. Telling people not to speed when they have this potential is like giving a kid a full bag of Halloween candy and saying, "Eat only half of it."

As long as we have fuel for the vehicles we drive, we'll be

tempted to go too fast and will feel frustrated with the proper pace of things, which hasn't changed in a hundred years.

"To remind myself what this proper pace is," says Kent Dawson, "I've set up an 'island of sanity.' This is a circle with my home at its center. Its radius is the distance I can travel on foot, either by running or walking. I don't use a car to move within this island, only to go outside of it. Within its boundaries, things must move at a gentle and unhurried pace because I have taken away the potential to hurry."

Ambition has its place. We sometimes have to reach beyond what we are, toward what we might become. We have to rush and strain to get there. But much of what we call being ambitious is nothing more than tugging against a leash which won't yield. No matter how fast it lets us go, we want to go faster. No matter where it lets us go, we want to go farther. We get nothing from this struggle except tired and angry.

The Cup Runneth Over

A RUNNER IS LIKE A CUP. His capacity to accept the stresses of running, racing, and living is fixed. At any one time, he can only take so much work. If he tries to pour in more than that amount, the excess just spills over the top. At best, he gains nothing. At worst, he dampens his spirit for doing new work.

Most runners are latent workaholics who are attracted to this sport because it seems to give free rein to that tendency. For that reason, most of us must learn about recovery as Dan Cahill did—the hard way.

The professional physical educator had for years talked about leading a balanced life, and he seemed to have his own life in good balance. Yet he now says, "I feel like a minister who suddenly realizes his son is a juvenile delinquent."

He explains, "I almost made 30 years of running without any serious problems. But since turning 40 (several years ago), I have been most competitive in my running and have won numerous Masters-division events. I have collected more trophies and medals in the last few years than in the previous 25. My ego has been on a continuous high. However . . ."

However, Dan fell into a familiar trap. The more he won, the more he wanted to win, and the harder he worked for it. He went past his capacity. There were other stresses not directly connected to running, but tensions don't conveniently stop at the border of their cause. They mix and flow freely, finding expression everywhere.

Cahill's attitude was, "If I plan my work well, stay in top physical condition and work hard, nothing can bother me."

Wrong.

He says that "in a period of approximately 12 months, all sorts of tensions hit me. I didn't realize the full impact until the end of the year. In December, I came down with my first serious injury in many years and was on the brink of a nervous breakdown. I developed numerous symptoms and spent many hours in doctors' offices trying to discover what was wrong."

Here he defends running. He says his "excellent physical condition was the only thing that prevented me from having a complete breakdown."

His running, and the soul-searching that his time on the roads allows, probably showed him the way out of his troubles: "I am now fully aware of what I have done to myself. I am practicing a series of relaxation techniques on a daily basis. I am running with the fitness joggers. I am sleeping nine or 10 hours per night. I am not going to run any marathons in the foreseeable future, and all other races will

be done at an 80-percent level. I have delegated some responsibility (at work) to other staff members and work
normal hours, never taking anything home to work on in the
evening."

He adds, "I have learned that when the floodgates open,
one should temper those stressors which are controllable.
The others will drive you bananas if you don't. It is the total
cumulative effect of stress that is dangerous."

Q

Quiet Qualities

In a quieter and more innocent age, the book *Thoughts on the Run* called this a sport for thinkers:

"Few come to it looking for long stretches of contemplation and meditation. But soon after starting, everyone sees he's faced with empty minutes and miles. There aren't any mental crutches to occupy his time—no television, newspapers, books, magazines, rarely any conversing with companions. He's alone with his thoughts. The experience can take him in several directions—to the fear of the strange and lonely silence, to boredom with the sameness of each mile, or to deep and concentrated thinking that has become rare in this hurried and harried age. Happily, most runners eventually arrive at the deep-thinking stage—and like it."

Rewriting these lines 12 years later, three changes must be made. First, "thinking-*man's* sport" obviously is outdated

117

wording; women finally share it equally. Second, we now know that the *non-thinking* which running allows is probably more important than the deep thinking; this is a time for head-clearing—a healthy kind of brain-washing.

The third change is an adverse one: Running is no longer naturally quiet. Its decibel level has climbed dramatically, both because more runners want to intrude on your time alone and because advertisers want to sell you their noise-makers.

Computer-age technology, combined with age-old sales techniques, now offer us what one ad calls "a way to make running fun again." It comes in a small package, suitable for wearing on a run. The radio-tape player dangles at the waist, connected to stereo earphones. It also connects you to the strident voices that runners refreshingly escaped in pre-cassette days.

The run can still be quiet, but you have to try harder now to keep it that way. Set aside one hour in 24 that is yours alone. Guard it jealously against all intruders, human or electronic. In all of your other waking hours, your head is being cluttered with the information, opinions, and de-mands of others. Keep this one hour as your time to remove that clutter instead of piling up more.

Leaving the Highway

Despite all the talk about Eugene, Oregon, being the "running capital"—the closest place to a runner's paradise here on earth—it is still a city. It holds more than 100,000 people and the traffic they produce, resulting in some clogged streets.

One is 30th Avenue. It connects the southeastern part of Eugene with a community college and an interstate high-

way. Leo Caponi lives just above 30th. To get almost anywhere on a run from home, he has to spend a mile or more on
this four-lane avenue. Since his running time matches going-
to-work/school time, he is used to seeing 30th at its worst.

"I know this is a sacrilege," Caponi says, "but I've started
driving places to run to avoid this street and its traffic." Leo
can think of no better use for his car than to haul him to his
recreation. By driving the busy streets, he can avoid them
when he runs.

"I run only about 45 minutes a day," he says. "Of that 45,
I spent five to 10 minutes on the near-freeway. I used up
most of the remaining time running through residential
neighborhoods, so I could take a short lap around a park or a
cemetery or some other quiet place.

"It makes a lot more sense—seeing as how an $8000 hunk
of metal with a full tank of gas sits in my garage—to drive to
places where I can spend *all* the time running in peace."

The only thing keeping Leo from doing this sooner was
the conviction that a runner never drives anywhere to start
a run. He drives to work, drives to the grocery store, drives
five miles for an ice-cream cone—but he never made a habit
of starting a run from his car. The incessant traffic finally
drove him into seclusion.

"My first thought was to head for the country," he says.
"The first week of testing my drive-and-run plan, I parked
at the edge of town and ran into the hills. The scenery may
have looked fine, but I never got a chance to see much of it.
I was too busy fearing for my life. Roads narrow in the
country, and traffic doubles in speed. I almost became a hood
ornament on a pickup or two."

Leo is now satisfied with places that are empty enough so
he never has to dodge cars. Serenity comes first; scenery is a
bonus: "I don't mind driving five or ten minutes to get to
places like Pre's Trail, since they make my runs 100 percent
more satisfying."

Run Softly, Run Tall

Runners pass judgment on every other passing runner. We do this partly according to how they dress (nylon warm-ups mean veteran; gray sweats with cotton shorts on the outside spell rookie), and partly by how fast they go (if one passes you, he's a pro; if you pass him, he's a jogger).

Nothing establishes a stronger first impression than running form. In some ways, style is as individual as a fingerprint. Each runner has his own distinctive marks. But the ways people run fall into two main categories:

> • Those who run *off* the ground—who seem to use the earth as a springboard for keeping themselves airborne.
> • Those who run *on* the ground—who shuffle or tiptoe along the surface as if they might fly off into space by breaking contact for too long.

One runner moves boldly, the other timidly. One runs as if the ground is a friend, the other as if it is an enemy trying to break him.

"I used to be the first kind of runner," says Leo Caponi. "No one runs the fast miles I once did by being afraid to spring from the earth. But years of wear and tear have made me more fragile and afraid. I finally woke up to that fact while running on Pre's Trail, a people-watching mecca."

As Leo watched the passing parade, it struck him: "'I'm not one of them,' I thought, as a group of hotshots from the University of Oregon bounded past. 'I'm one of *them*,' meaning the timid shufflers who run on stiff legs and flat feet that barely clear the ground."

He now suffered from what writer-runner Mike Tymn defined as "clinicitis." When asked why the runners at the Honolulu Marathon Clinic didn't ever lift their knees, Tymn answered, "They are required to carry canteens and check their dehydration levels every 100 yards. The excess consumption of liquids is thought to cause edema in the knees, which in turn keeps the individual moving at a 'safe' pace."

Tymn was kidding, of course. And these apprentice marathoners can be pardoned for shuffling; they haven't yet learned how to run fast.

"I don't have that excuse," says Caponi. "I ran fast from day one—and kept pushing almost daily for the next eight years. I did springboard-type running for all that time, then slipped gradually into the shuffling style."

Leo Caponi had been driving all day. The nice thing about a long drive is that it opens empty hours to be filled with thoughts. The not-so-nice thing is that the thoughts aren't always pleasant.

"As I pushed the car up Interstate Five from sunny California into the rain and gloom of Oregon, my thinking came round to how tired I was of running on sore feet. They'd hurt constantly for more than a year. I'd cut runs short and all but quit racing. *Do something!* I told myself. But what?

"An answer came that same afternoon as I ran on Pre's Trail. Even more than normally, the runs here open me up to good ideas. One jumped into my head about a half-hour into the run: *Don't protect!*"

Caponi felt himself running like an arthritic old man: "I was stiff-legged, flat-footed, short-strided. My feet felt like two clenched fists. I ran this way thinking I was reducing pain, but I may have been adding to it."

Running this way is jarring, jamming, and tightening to the feet and lower legs. They act as ramrods instead of the shock-absorbers they are meant to be.

Leo whispered new instructions to himself: *Lift the knees at pushoff . . . Flex the ankles . . . Spring from the big toes . . . Land with the knees slightly bent . . . Fall a little farther forward on the feet.*

The most obvious results of this new style—or rather, a

return to an old one—were a bouncier, "taller," slightly faster way of running. But the more subtle results were the ones that Caponi liked more.

He says, "The way I've been running the last many years has only seemed to 'protect' my sore feet. In fact, it has slammed them harder against the ground than it should have. I haven't been giving myself the shock-absorption that nature intended on footstrike.

"The only time I've run correctly is when I've had no choice. This happens in races or on hills. Once speed picks up to racing rate, I'm forced to land with a flexed knee, to spring with the ankle, to roll forward off the big toe. It hasn't been by chance that I've felt my best—in the feet and lower legs, anyway—during and right after races.

"Hill running also forces a more natural style. Uphills require more drive and lift from the knees and ankles, more stretch from the full foot. Downhill running requires flexed knees; otherwise, it can be a shattering experience. I've had days during the dark year when I couldn't run without limping on flat surfaces. And yet as soon as the ground tilted up or down, the pain eased."

The hills were trying to tell Leo something, just as the races were. They weren't saying that the hard work of climbing or pushing the pace was inherently better for him than comfortable running. They were telling him that the *style* of harder, faster running may be the natural one for all terrains and efforts.

PRANCE. If there's a single word that defines this style, it is prancing. Not running like a drum major at a Saturday afternoon football game, but running as if you're rather proud of yourself. This prancing has three trigger-points:

1. *Foot*—Make full use of it. The argument for years has been heel-running versus toe-running. Both sides are right in what they promote and wrong in what they

deny. A good style involves *both* heels and toes, especially the big toe. Land at midfoot, rock gently back onto the heel, then roll forward onto the toes, leaving the ground from the big one.

2. *Ankle*—Flex it. Use it to get bounce from the ground. The more rigid the ankle is, the more jarring the contact with the ground will be. Famed coach Arthur Lydiard has said that some of the most vital muscles in the body are those controlling the ankle. They determine how softly you land and how strongly you push off. Think "flex" and "snap" as the ankle does its two jobs.

3. *Knee*—Lift it. A one-sentence lesson in the physics of running: the lift of the knee controls the fall of the foot. If the knees ride low and rigid, in other words, so will the feet. You'll get a flat-footed, jolting, awkward stride of the type Mike Tymn called "clinicitis." Pick up the knee and bend it.

The result of all this is taller, bolder running. That much is obvious. But the less visible part may be more important. This is not what you see but what you hear—or rather, *don't* hear. Good running is quiet running. What you don't hear when the foot meets the ground is not likely to hurt you.

R

Racing Among Ourselves

A Place for Everyone

THE REAL BATTLE IS WON. The public has come to accept running as something which can't be chased away with stares and insults. Running still isn't a widely loved act and probably never will be. It is too far removed from the mainstream of motorized America for that. But few runners need to be loved; being ignored is good enough.

The battle to be ignored is won. The forerunners had to make themselves targets of physical and verbal abuse so that everyone could run easier. But that kind of outside harassment is the exception rather than the rule now.

Some runners have battled for so long, though, that they can't stop battling. Without an ignorant public to fight, they now pick fights with other runners.

Track and Field News, the magazine of record in this sport, carried a letter from a reader who doesn't like the direction running has taken.

Gene Liss of St. Louis wrote, "I think the jogging and marathon craze is in some ways hurting real running. Nobody runs a 220 or a two-miler anymore. It is just some damn dentist bragging about 'completing a marathon.' You ask him how fast, and he answers, 'Four hours and 37 minutes.' Now is that really running? Perseverance, maybe; running, not really."

Don't blame *T&FN* for these comments. Publications don't create opinion; they reflect and report it. If magazines are carrying more bad news and views on the "running boom," it's because more runners think the new masses have polluted their running environment. Theirs is not a new outlook but a wish to return to an old one, a view not too different from the prevailing one in other American sports.

These people would have us believe that running is meant to be practiced only by the young and the talented. Women are admitted only reluctantly and always in second-class status. The schools act as minor-league training grounds. Survivors at that level move on to college, and the few athletes who excel there graduate into the professional ranks. Anyone who can't keep climbing the competitive ladder is forced to take a seat in front of the TV or to buy a ticket in the stadium.

Road running grew up under a different, perhaps unique, set of rules. It didn't sprout from the survival-of-the-fittest system of school sports. Until recently, it had no professional level. From the time the road sport exploded, the very old and very young, the female and the slow were welcome. Perhaps this was why it exploded.

The operating philosophy of the roads was expressed more than a decade ago by a trackman-turned-road-runner who said he would rather see 10,000 people running a mile at whatever pace they could handle—and no one watching them run—than to have the 10,000 in the stands watching one man run 3:50.

There wasn't room for that many runners on the track, so

they took to the road. This became the sandlot of running, where people of all shapes and speeds could play instead of watch. Anyone could take pride in his or her efforts, no matter how humble.

What we are seeing now is not a civil war among types of runners—not even an organized campaign against the less fit or fast. Rather, it is a subtle shift in philosophy, back toward the more traditional values of sports.

The shift is away from "everyone is welcome" and toward "only the best should compete, and the rest should stay out of their way." Road racing doesn't fit into this trend toward old-style thinking, so the defenders of quality over quantity use this branch of the sport for target practice.

They say track is the true sport, road running a cheap imitation and that the boom in the latter has hurt the former. Support for this theory has come from an unexpected source: Craig Virgin. An Associated Press report made the versatile runner seem to take an anti-road stand.

"I think that road racing could hurt track and field here in the end," Virgin said. "Road racing is where the time, attention, and money are now going in the United States. I think some of the better distance runners in track and field are being drawn away to road racing."

These comments sound strange, coming from one who raced an American-record 10,000, won the International Cross-Country title, and placed second in the Boston Marathon within a 10-month period.

Virgin did say later in the interview that he would "continue to participate in track, road racing, and cross-country. I think all three can complement each other." But the writer already had made his point that the roads are depleting the track. The logic is shaky.

At the top, relatively few runners divide their time between the specialties—let alone give up the old one for the new. Those who do diversify don't seem to suffer much for it. When he is healthy, Virgin beats almost everyone in all arenas. Grete Waitz's track and cross-country work hasn't slumped since she started setting world marathon records.

Great running is great running, no matter what its surface. The same can be said for a great runner, no matter where he or she runs.

Most road runners, however, aren't from the Virgin-Waitz class. Most of them never ran track or cross-country in school, and few of them ever will enter these more traditional disciplines. They wouldn't be racing at all if the roads weren't open to them.

Yet as these new runners' interests mature, they come to appreciate how well a Virgin or a Waitz runs. They follow the careers of the superstars on and off the roads. Today's new road runner is tomorrow's track fan. He or she may soon contribute to the biggest wave of track interest ever seen.

Road racing might also push more new runners onto the track than it draws away. Marty Liquori thinks this is happening now. He said the young Americans' sweeps of the 1500, 10,000, and steeplechase in the 1981 U.S.-Russian track meet were products of "the running boom sweeping the country."

Liquori's opinion has changed. A few years ago, he said that the emphasis on long training, road racing, and fun-running was hurting young runners. He thought no high-school miler had broken four minutes since the 1960s because none trained hard enough any more.

Time has shown Marty to be wrong, and he admits it now. The four-minute mile remains unbroken because high schoolers put more stress on laying a base for future success. The results show up as early as college. U.S. winners Jim Spivey, Mark Nenow, and John Gregorek all were college age when they beat the Soviets in 1981.

Their success fits the "pyramid theory": The broader a runner's base of endurance, the higher he can push his peak of speed. The speed-from-the-start training system of the

1960s produced a rare Liquori or Jim Ryun, and lots of early dropouts. The endurance-based system of the '80s yields strong and fast runners in depth.

The success of the country's runners as a whole also fits the pyramid pattern. The huge numbers of people running at ground level support a peak higher than it has ever been before. The best of us stand on the shoulders of the rest of us, and this effect extends from the roads to the track.

The roads may contribute in other, more material ways to track. If the road boom has created runners who wouldn't have existed otherwise, it also has created businesses. The Athletic Attic and Phidippides chains probably wouldn't be here without the boom. Nike and New Balance wouldn't be shoemaking giants. Sponsors like Perrier and Pepsi wouldn't be attracted to events with 25 runners.

None of the road-racing riches have been drawn *from* track. But some of them are flowing and more will flow *to* track as runners and businessmen see that road and track are part of the same whole.

The second argument of the new critics is that trackmen and women are the true athletes, road runners the imposters. The assumption here is that road runners are frustrated athletes who have failed at all other sports, including perhaps the conventional side of this sport. Critics say these runners envy the fastest ones and imagine they are like them by plodding out longer and longer distances without ever getting faster. The *Track and Field News* letter writer called this perseverance, not running.

In fact, most long-distance runners are too busy with their own work to worry about anyone else's. Half of them know who the winners are and admire them without envying them. The other half don't know and don't care who's in front.

No runner is so humble that he can't feel some pride in a race well run, meaning finishing in expected time or better.

In every race, runners far back in the pack leap and shout and cry for joy as they finish. This joy has nothing to do with imagining they are breaking the tape. They know just who they are and just what they've done. Others might have done it faster, but no one else could have finished for them.

Road racing has opened this sport to common folks who wouldn't otherwise have had a place to be athletic. These common folks have made road racing what it is. They built it up from the bottom. They wrote its rules. To say now that they don't belong on the roads unless they play by the rules of track is arrogant and cruel. To say that a slower runner has no right to feel proud of his work is one step from saying that only the best should run; the rest should watch.

We who ran the roads before they got crowded welcome the elite from track who have joined us here. We only ask them never to say that we and our ways of thinking and running don't belong.

DOUBLE DUTY

NOT LONG AGO, putting on a road race was a simple and often primitive matter. A runner who wasn't in much of a hurry would start the watch, then hide it in the bushes before chasing off after his friends. The first one done would dive into the bushes, check his time and become the timer for everyone else. The second finisher would pick up a clipboard and be the day's scorer. Finishing early had its rewards but also its obligations.

We didn't need to stand in line to sign up for a race then, because there weren't enough of us to form a line. We didn't need to wear numbers, because everyone knew everyone else. All we needed was someone to check and write down results. We runners shared the clerical responsibilities.

Race management moved from the bushes to the computer within a few years. Some of us who started as bushmen haven't yet caught up with the new way of doing things. But all of us admit that today's races with 10,000 people can't be run as simply as the old ones with 10.

What we really miss about the old days is the feeling that runners have a duty to help each other.

Running attracts recruits partly because this is one place where a person can take control of himself. As a runner takes control over his movement, he learns that true energy flows from within, not from Arab oil fields. He sees that injuries and illnesses may be a doctor's responsibility, but health and fitness are his own.

We runners take charge of our everyday running. We decide if, when, where, and how we'll do it. No one else makes us run, watches us run, or cares if we run or not. We do it all ourselves, because *we* know and we care. In this sense, running is an adult activity.

But many of these same runners go back to acting like spoiled children when they race. They give control to the officials and expect to be pampered. They complain quickly and loudly when the organization isn't perfect. And races seldom are perfect when two chronic problems, the crush of runners and the shortage of help, collide.

It would be easy to predict that races as we know them might soon be extinct for lack of officials. Wrong. We'll have races as long as runners want them. The question is, what kind of races? There are three possibilities:

> • *The Fun-Run Solution.* This is racing reduced to its simplest terms: no sign-ups, no entry fees, no numbers, no splits, no recorded results, no prizes; just send the runners off along a more-or-less marked course and shout times at them at the end. One official can handle it all, more or less.
> • *The Professional Solution.* A sponsor pays for the services of a race director, who in turn re-

cruits paid helpers to time, score, and guide the
runners. Everything gets done right—for a price
which the runners ultimately pay.

• *The Secret Solution.* A runner from Oregon
says, "We have a group called 'OUR'—O for the
state, Underground Runners. We have races,
we have members, and we have smallness—all
the things old-timers want. And we have done it
simply: we just don't advertise. Members are
obtained by word of mouth only. When a member joins, he or she is given a packet containing
a race schedule with dates, times, and locations
of races, and a detailed description of each
course. The description is important, because
the race courses are not marked. Each member
is expected to know it."

Each solution has obvious practical merit—simplicity,
quality, or smallness. But runners sometimes want more
than times, or balk at having high administrative costs passed
on to them, or don't want races treated like private clubs.

Another, better solution would retain the quality of races
while keeping them cheap and open. This would involve
runners giving back to the sport a portion of what they take
from it. For instance, we would volunteer to hold a stopwatch or clipboard at one race for every 10 that we run. This
way, the pool of helpers would grow as races do.

Every time we take, we owe a little bit. We'd all race
smoother if each of us paid back that debt at the rate of
10 percent.

S

Stopping in Time

SEVERAL YEARS AGO, *Runner's World* magazine published a marathon training plan. It told beginners how to get ready for their first long race and how to finish it without too much trauma. The schedule drew fire from two directions.

Dr. Jack Scaff, director of the Honolulu Marathon Clinic (which has its own schedule and a 98-percent race-completion rate from its thousands of graduates), said the program made people run too much. They recovered too little between runs and got hurt too often.

Manfred Steffny, a German Olympian and his country's leading running writer, criticized the schedule for the opposite reason. He said it didn't offer enough running. A beginner couldn't hope to find enough background training in it to complete a marathon.

Several hundred satisfied users of the *RW* program say that both Scaff and Steffny were wrong. Most of the runners

132

who tried this training program survived it. Nearly all of those who started a marathon with this background finished it. But the author of that program still had a confession to make.

"I'm a fraud," he admitted with a smile during a talk at a pre-race clinic. "Here you are getting ready to run a marathon tomorrow. Many of you may have used a schedule I wrote. But do I use it? No. I haven't done a marathon—or even wanted to think about one—in a long time. Do you know what I raced most recently? Ten kilometers. Not even an honest 10-K with hills, but a sissy race on the track."

Shortly after that, he faced a crowd of beginners. The goal in this group was to finish a marathon within a year of starting to run, and most of them were close to succeeding.

The speaker said, "Do you know how long it took me to get up the nerve to run a marathon? Nine years. And do you know I'm the only one in this room tonight who doesn't care if he ever runs a marathon again? Ten kilometers is far enough. My current crusade is to promote that as the perfect running and racing distance."

The marathon is a good place to begin, but not to stay. Beginners need goals, and this long run is a good one. It is a sneaky way to get them addicted to running, because its training takes them right away into the addictive distances —those needing 30 to 60 minutes to complete. At first, the marathon gives them more satisfaction than any short race could.

Almost anyone can finish 10 kilometers on a few weeks' training, but almost no one has enough speed that soon to run this race fast. So 10-K doesn't seem like much of an accomplishment early on. But to a beginner, finishing a marathon at any pace is like climbing Everest.

The evidence from Jack Scaff's Honolulu Marathon Clinic shows clearly that most runners take only a few weeks to progress to an hour of running. Few of them get hurt or quit the program. Few fail to finish the marathon. Few quit running after the marathon is behind them.

But back to the claim of a few paragraphs ago: The marathon is a nice place to visit, but few racers can live there. Most of those who try either don't truly race the distance or hurt themselves in the attempt.

With due respect to the wonderful efforts of the people in the marathon clinics, few of them *race* the distance. They *survive* it, taking four or five or more hours to finish. After finishing one marathon, they probably would be better off to back down in distance and to race for speed.

One autumn, a group of seasoned runners in Illinois were working together on their marathon speed. Most had times near three hours and wanted to go faster. By the next spring, none of the five was running. One had a back injury, one an arch problem, one a groin pull, and so on.

Tom Brighton, their friend who watched this attrition, says, "I'm not laughing and pointing any fingers at them. I'm only offering sympathy from one who has gone their way before them—not only once but many times. I got hurt a lot when I ran marathons. The racing itself hurt me, and so did the training for it. It's amazing how healthy I've stayed since I quit racing this far—and at the other extreme of all-out speed in the mile."

Brighton's answer to people who now ask why he doesn't race miles is, "I like to compete too much to finish it so quickly. If I'm going to go to the trouble of racing, driving an hour or more to get there, standing around for another hour before the race starts, then taking two more hours afterward to talk it over and drive home, I want the racing to last longer than five minutes."

The mile is a mad dash. It relates no more to what Tom does every day than a casual drive through the country does to a drag race. The mile is less than 20 percent of his usual distance and nearly 50 percent faster. To prepare for a mile, he would have to do regular speedwork and accept its risks.

His answer to those who ask why he doesn't run marathons is, "I like to race too much to run them. If I ran marathons, I would have to give up short races in favor of long training runs for a couple of months before each 26-miler. I would have to give up more racing while recovering from marathons. This normally takes at least a month. If I ran four marathons a year, I would use up the whole 12 months just getting ready for and getting over them—with no time left for any other racing."

For someone who doesn't care to suffer daily or to delay gratification, the perfect run is about 10 kilometers. The perfect race is that distance, too. Runs and races come easiest and most efficiently at 10-K, giving the most benefit for the least effort.

Anyone who didn't run or race might think otherwise. Good sense would seem to show that the first step comes cheapest, and each succeeding one carries a higher price. But anyone who has run more than a month or raced more than once knows better. The first steps are always hard—hard every day because of the effort involved in breaking inertia; hard in races because so much violent activity must be packed into so little time.

Ten-kilometer runs and races take care of the warm-up and spread out the violence before replacing them with the strains of long-distance work. Runs and races at this transition point between short and long are as pleasant as they ever get.

It is no accident, then, that eight in every 10 races nationwide go this distance. The race is a natural for both popularity and frequency. Its perfection takes many forms:

> • *Time*—Almost everyone finishes it in 30 to 60 minutes, which makes it long enough but not too long.
> • *Pace*—Not too fast or too slow; it's a true race without being a mad dash.

• *Training*—Nothing special is needed, since most runners go this far every day and this fast every week or so in races.
• *Recovery*—It doesn't take long; using the standard one-day-per-mile formula, a 10-K race each week is possible.

This distance makes a good home for runners who have gone to the extreme of speed or distance, or both. This home base may not be as thrilling as the exotic locales at the extremes. But this is a place where we can settle down, relax, live comfortably, and avoid much of the rat-racing that very fast and very long travel involves.

GIVE YOURSELF A BREAK

IN THAT YEAR OF THE MILE, 1981, the most amazing of the milers was not Sebastian Coe or Steve Ovett. They merely did what was expected of them—a little more dramatically than anyone thought they would, perhaps, but not beyond their awesome potential.

Todd Harbour didn't think he belonged with them, at least not that year. He had run quite well as a 21-year-old in 1980, but he'd never broken 3:58 for the mile. And early 1981 hadn't gone well for him.

A calf-muscle pull and sympathetic pains in a hamstring had reduced Harbour to 4:11 miling in the spring. He had just about written off his season by then and had eased up on his training, resting four or five days at a time. The injury suddenly healed. He placed second in the NCAA 1500, then dropped a place but ran faster at TAC.

These races sharpened Todd for the most amazing time in The Year of the Mile. He improved by eight seconds with his 3:50.34 at Oslo.

It might be written that Todd Harbour improved this much that summer "despite his injury." But an equal argument might be made that being hurt *helped* him. Because of that calf injury, Harbour was able to do less training and racing during the college season—the March-to-May period when runners double and triple in search of team points and relay victories. Todd's forced rest kept him hungry. He came back fresh and frustrated, put in six good weeks of work and ran the race of his life.

Stories like this aren't unusual. Steve Plasencia hurt an achilles tendon in 1980 and went into surgery that Christmas Eve. He didn't start training again until the next March. However, six months later in Europe Steve raced 5000 meters in 13:25, a nine-second improvement on his best pre-injury time.

Plasencia says this first serious injury of his career taught him several important lessons. One was "the self-control we need as a basis for long-term, healthy, productive running." His most valuable lesson, though, was one that all runners are slow to learn: There are times when we train best *by not running*. We progress by stopping and letting our bodies catch up with the work being demanded of them.

Any pain usually means we've already overworked. Additional work usually just makes the pain worse. Harbour and Plasencia didn't improve until they were forced to slow down or stop. They had such a backlog of training, however, that they returned from their layoffs—a pause for Harbour but a major vacation for Plasencia—stronger than ever.

The lesson here for all runners may be that we need an occasional training holiday. We might be wise not to wait for nature to demand it with an injury or an illness, but to take it voluntarily.

Jeff Galloway, an Olympian at 10,000 meters in 1972, suggests a plan of this type. Jeff has learned that he can only run hard about one day a week. So he saves a race, a long

run, or a speed session for that day, then fills the time between with gentler runs.

Jeff also knows that he can't improve indefinitely. He has
to slack off once in a while to pull himself out of "fatigue
debt." The formula he has come up with for himself is one
easy week in every four.

Galloway doesn't take that week completely off. He's
too much of a running addict for that. But he does cut his
training by half, scheduling no long or fast runs. He says he
comes back stronger than if he had pushed through that
week at normal mileage and pace.

Alternating hard and easy days has been a standard training practice for at least a decade. Bill Bowerman found early
in his coaching career that runners improved fastest and
most if they mixed work days with recovery days.

What Galloway proposes is an extension of "hard-easy"
to longer periods of time: recovery *weeks* mixed in among
work weeks. The theory also applies to months, seasons, and
even years.

For Everything, a Season

Tom Osler is one of the brightest thinkers in running, even
though he doesn't normally appear on the sport's "guru
lists." He pioneered the modern training book with his *Conditioning of Distance Runners* in 1966 and expanded on its
themes in his *Serious Runner's Handbook*. They never
reached the audiences they deserved. The first came out too
early, before there was much of an audience to reach. The
second came out too late, when it had too much competition
for attention. So Osler remains one of the great unsung
geniuses of running.

Tom was so slow and thick-legged as an early runner that
his friends called him Turtle. Yet he stretched his five-

minute-mile ability into national championships at distances from 25 kilometers to 50 miles. He broke 2½ hours for the marathon when that time was still national-class.

More importantly, Osler thought about running and wrote out his analyses. One of his long-buried pieces has to do with seasonal ups and downs.

"One can rarely maintain a high-performance level for more than three months," he begins. "Heavy racing must therefore be terminated after about three months or when symptoms of energy depletion are first observed."

Osler found that each of his years fell neatly into two cycles lasting six months apiece. Each cycle held a high period of about three months and a low of the same length. He got his best results and stayed healthiest if he pushed his racing and race-like training at the high times and avoided them during the lows.

The highs and lows might be made to occur at any time of year, Osler says. For instance, a runner could peak in January and again in July. But the half-year patterns remain fairly consistent. As surely as one hits a high in, say, the first month, he will hit bottom in the fourth. If the PRs come in January, the discouraging times and then the disabling ailments follow in April. A runner can enhance the former and avoid the latter by cooperating with these natural cycles.

The traditional highs came in spring and fall, the lows in winter and summer. Before road racing grew up in the U.S. as a sport for all seasons, before there were summer all-comers track meets, we ran track from March to May and cross-country from September to November. We ran easily, if at all, between racing seasons.

No one would want the sport to go back to those old days when only the best could run (no slow, no very old or very young, no women runners), and they could do it for only brief periods each year.

The *chance* to race year-round is a wonderful advance. But it puts the responsibility on us now to *choose* which seasons to race and when to avoid racing. The opportunities have improved, but the rules haven't changed. It's still a very rare runner who can race well indefinitely.

Whether there is anything to Tom Osler's three-months-high/three-months-low theory or not, it still makes good sense to run with the seasons of the year. The best weather and best races come in the spring and fall, and the least attractive racing occurs in the cold and hot months. Schedule your year to take advantage of its natural ups and downs.

In the words of Ecclesiastes, "To everything, there is a season and a time for every purpose under heaven . . . a time to kill and a time to heal, a time to break down and a time to build up."

T

Tactics and Tricks

LITTLE THINGS MEAN A LOT

DICK BEARDSLEY, the Minnesotan who may one day hold the world marathon record, is a refreshingly open young man. He admits to superstitions that most runners of 2:08 class would keep secret.

Beardsley tells a story on himself. It isn't the one about spitting twice on the starting line and then wiping the spit away with his foot. Nor is it the one about sliding his wedding ring off and on exactly four times within one minute of the start. He does these things, but there is another story.

He worries that "the men in the white coats will come and cart me away if I tell this." Then he goes ahead with the telling.

Dick insisted on racing in the same shoes, shorts, and singlet that served him well in his last good races. Trouble was, he had run so many good races in one year that time had come for a change.

He fretted over his decision to abandon the proven uniform before his biggest race. Then he found a solution at the last minute.

The Beardsleys were staying within sight of the finish line. As they left the motel, Dick told his wife, Mary, "Wait here. I'll be right back. I forgot something."

He rushed inside—and hung his clothes and set his shoes in the window.

"If I couldn't wear them," he says, "then at least they could watch how I did."

The old uniform must have approved. It saw Beardsley run the second-fastest marathon time ever done by an American.

It's comforting to know that runners at this level worry as much about seemingly silly little acts as lesser runners do.

One of them said after hearing the Beardsley story, "I always knew that the sheer bulk of a marathon terrified me. But I didn't think a Dick Beardsley had the same nervous reaction or dealt with it as I did."

Harold Murphy has a hard time even now, after more than 30 completed marathons, conceiving of how he can go that far on foot.

"Twenty-six miles, 385 yards doesn't look so big when I see it written out," he says. "It takes less than a line. I can say it in one breath. The enormity of a marathon only comes clear when I see it laid out in a straight line."

No demonstration of that was more graphic than the one Murphy saw before his first marathon. His debut was at Boston. The tradition then, as now, was to board buses in front of the Prudential Center in downtown Boston and ride out to the starting line in suburban Hopkinton. Then, unlike now, the driver rather sadistically took the runners over the exact marathon route in reverse.

What impressed Harold the most was not its hills or its scenery, but its distance. "I have to run all this!" he kept mumbling to himself.

"I ran it all and was happy enough with the way it went to run dozens more marathons. But I've never again looked at a marathon course in advance, in total. I don't want to see all of the road that lies ahead.

"I now go into all races blind, without seeing exactly where they'll take me. I just follow the people in front of me, follow the direction signs and run from split marker to split marker."

The way to run a long race is to break it up into little pieces and to concentrate on them one at a time. Likewise, the way to avoid some of the big worries that any race carries with it is to concentrate on little acts, rituals, in other words—wearing the same clothes and shoes from race to race, or at least hanging them in a window to "watch," as Dick Beardsley does; running an unseen course as Harold Murphy does.

These are neutral acts. They don't interfere with the race, or the runners would have dropped them the first time they cost a few seconds. They give little direct aid, either. This fact separates true rituals from profitable moves like a well-timed warm-up, the right pacing plan, or enough of the right kinds of drinks taken en route.

Rituals are games we play which have great meaning but serve no purpose other than as safety valves for tension.

BEFORE THE RACE

RACE-DAY RITUALS of a well-practiced neurotic, who once wrote that racing is "like knowing you are about to be mugged. You cling to friends for comfort as you wait for the blow to land." His rituals are those friends:

> • He wakes up at least two hours before race time—even when the event starts right outside his door, even when time-zone changes make him get out of bed at three A.M., body time. He's

convinced he needs that long to clear his head and limber up his legs, even when it means losing sleep.

• He brews a cup of weak tea and drinks it straight. He doesn't take it for nourishment or a caffeine kick, but to insure that his bladder and bowels will flush properly in the next two hours. He eats nothing.

• He shaves and showers *before* running. Some runners like to go into a race feeling scruffy; they say this makes them feel mean. But meanness isn't part of this one's act; cleanness is. It tricks him into the bright-eyed, I-can-take-on-anything mood he's normally only in *after* everyday runs.

• He puts on one shirt and carries another. The first is a T-shirt to wear while warming up; he chooses one from a successful past race (his version of the Beardsley ritual) but *never* uses the shirt given at the current event. The second shirt is a singlet which he never wears except when racing.

• He arrives at the race site promptly an hour before starting time. This allows him to check in and to swap tales with fellow liars about, "I'm only in it for a workout," and, "I've been hurt and will be lucky to finish."

• He avoids setting foot onto the race course until it counts. All preparations are done elsewhere.

• He starts warming up precisely a half-hour before the gun: 15 minutes of easy running (or simply walking if the race is to be extra-long), then a few more minutes of stretching and striding.

• He changes into his racing singlet. It is chosen not to draw attention to himself but to help make him anonymous. The singlet bears no identification. The number pinned on it is trimmed of any advertising messages.

• He lines up in mid-pack, *never* right on the white line. He punches on his wristwatch timer not at the gun but when he crosses the line or starts running, whichever comes last.

• He plans to make his first mile his slowest, the last his fastest and to speed up gradually in between. Few runners of his ability want to start that slowly, and few are able to stay with him later as he accelerates. This, too, fits into the plan. He hates to match strides with anyone during races. That encourages conversation, and to him a race isn't a moving cocktail party.

AFTER THE RACE

JOHN STEINBECK'S BOOK *Travels with Charley* is more an essay on the nature of all trips than a travelogue on the country he toured.

He writes, "My own journey started long before I left and was over before I returned," and, "One goes not so much to see but to tell afterward."

A race is like that. The limits of racing success are drawn before the race starts—in the training you do and the mistakes you don't make before going to the line. Then the race pretty much runs itself. You go through it seeing little more than the finish line.

Steinbeck describes the sensation when he tells of his journey ending near the Continental Divide, where he quit seeing anything but his home in faraway New York.

"I was driving myself, pounding out the miles," he says. "The road became an endless stone ribbon, the hills obstructions, the trees green blurs, the people simply moving figures with heads but no faces."

Steinbeck might have been describing a race, for you race alone, no matter how large the field. No one can share your workload which becomes heavier the farther you go.

Racing is no fun while you're doing it. The fun comes from sharing the experience later.

The self-centered vision clears and the sharing starts as the finish line comes into view. Some runners tap hidden pools of energy to sprint the last few yards. This surge is more an all's-well-that-ends-well ritual than a move with meaning.

An alternate ritual is to let late sprinters pass without a challenge. Anyone who wants that badly to beat you out of 189th place can have that honor.

You race not so much to see but to tell afterward. The telling begins immediately, as you and the late kicker hang onto each other and say, "Nice work!" The post-race ritual prohibits a runner from saying anything uncomplimentary to another.

If you get a break in conversation, you slip away to change into a dry T-shirt, preferably the one from this race, and to do some cool-down running, walking and stretching. But if forced to choose between that activity and bragging about yourself, you skip the cool-down. Post-race chatter is a ritual not to be missed.

You linger at the finish line, talking to everyone who will listen for as long as they will listen. You even do some listening yourself if it will prolong this talking.

Later you'll go home and tell the race story to your diary. It always listens patiently and never protests that you brag too much.

But first comes food. The rituals of racing must include a meal, preferably shared with others who have raced. A pre-race carbohydrate binge is a hollow occasion, because all you can talk about is what you "might" or "hope to" do. That talk is always tinged with doubt. And that meal, taken in excess, can always return to haunt you the next morning. A carbo-*reloading* party carries no such worries.

As you eat, you glance frequently at the black watch on your wrist. Frozen in digital time are the minutes and seconds that you earned with your sweat. You indulge your pride for a full day after racing.

Not until you start to run again the next morning do you zero the watch. The wiping away of a result says that it is time to quit looking back at an old race and start looking ahead to a new run. This is the final—and perhaps most important—racing ritual.

U

Ultimate Winners

THE GUINNESS SYNDROME

OUR HEROES ARE THOSE RUNNERS who operate at the outer limits of speed and distance. You can either envy them for what they have and you don't, or admire them from a safe place without feeling any need to take their risks.

As thin a line separates heroism from tragedy as divides genius from insanity. The people who take the biggest chances run the biggest risks of stepping over those lines. The runners you know as heroic might just as easily be seen as tragic characters.

Doug Latimer wouldn't think of himself as a tragic figure, but others might. No one has approached the Western States 100-mile race with greater passion than Latimer. He could end his career happily if the last step he took was as a Western States winner. In 1979, he led the race for more than 15 hours before being passed with five miles to go. In 1980, leading by a half-hour at 83 miles, Doug was stopped

148

by cramps so bad that he screamed in pain. In 1981, he trained even harder than before, ran his fastest time over the Sierra Nevada trail, and had to settle for a winning tie.

Al Arnold has a similar one-sided affair with Mt. Whitney. The first time he tried to run from the floor of Death Valley to the peak of Whitney, Arnold quit after just 18 miles. He completed the 145-mile trip the second time but wasn't satisfied. He wanted to go round-trip. Al tried that one summer after training on a bike in a 170-degree sauna and by running up a mountain with 80 pounds on his back. The distance, desert, and mountain beat him anyway.

The yawning width of Canada didn't stop Terry Fox, nor did the fact that he had only one leg—and hadn't been much of a runner even before he lost it. Fox decided to run across his country to raise money for cancer research and to show what a cancer victim could do. He'd covered 3300 miles when a severe cough and chest pains forced him to stop. The long-dormant cancer had reactivated and invaded his lungs during the run.

While Latimer, Arnold, and Fox covered great distances in which mountains happened to be obstacles, John Link sought out the high places. He loved the Colorado Rockies and ran them daily. He was a pioneer in the esoteric sport of mountain racing. In 1979, Link slipped while running up Isolation Peak and fell to his death.

People who don't run might call some or all of these runners failures, or say they were foolish even to go to such lengths to prove that man has limits. We who also run call them heroes for showing what is possible. We might also appreciate them for warning us what not to try.

Be careful not to get sucked into the "Guinness Syndrome." This is the attitude, an increasingly common one in running, that the sport is worth practicing only if it keeps leading to new records.

This thinking seduces runners more than any other ath-

letes, because what we do is so measurable and comparable.
There are records for speed, distance, and now even altitude.
We can set records by age group, sex, and weight-class. If
we're good enough, we can break other runners' records. If
not, we can work against our own.

To a degree, chasing records is normal and healthy. *Time*
magazine essayist Frank Trippett writes, "It is easy to understand the performer's urge to do the improbable, the difficult, the unique, the best. Claiming a record—any record—
provides massage to the ego, varnish for the pride and a tick
of celebrity. . . .

"Now that society has become so proficient at keeping records as a way of celebrating the competitive trait, it is no
wonder that people get so carried away in the making and
breaking of them."

Trying for legitimate records isn't the problem. Getting
carried away in the pursuit of them is.

No one is more proficient at record-keeping than Norris
McWhirter, the Briton who with his late twin Ross started
the *Guinness Book of World Records*. No one gets more
carried away than somebody who tries to break into that
book.

Norris McWhirter says, "People are fascinated with extremes. They like to know what the steel brackets are around
a subject. It may be significant that the average snake is, let's
say, 4½ feet long. But it's somehow more interesting that the
longest one is a python measuring 32 feet and the shortest
is just a few inches—a worm, really.

"People crave delineation and points of reference. It's a
matter of orientation, but it's also part of the natural com-
petitiveness that most of us have."

By publishing records, the Guinness people have appealed
to the side of us which wants to compete well and be recognized for it. This has created what Jerry Kirshenbaum of
Sports Illustrated calls "Guinnessport," which has as its main
purpose "to crack the book's pages."

This push to set records divides those who attempt them into two groups:

> • *The heroes* who tiptoe along the line between heroism and tragedy in widely practiced events like running for speed and distance. As records progress, they get harder and harder to break—and leave more victims among the challengers.
> • *The weirdos* who practice what Norris McWhirter calls "ridiculous variations" of true sports. Writer Kirshenbaum says they dream up record attempts "that rely less on talent than on brass and tenacity."

Running now has both kinds. Every era has had runners who extended the limits of what was thought to be possible and have deserved to be praised for this. But now the Guinness era has made it possible for almost anyone with imagination to set some kind of record. We've never been closer to the time predicted by Andy Warhol when everyone gets to be a celebrity for 15 minutes.

Two related theories of running evolution:

1. Nothing changes. The sport simply runs through cycles. Every 50 years or so, it goes to extremes of distance. About 1880, there was a brief craze in six-day racing. The late 1920s was a time of transcontinental Bunion Derbies. Now we have Western States 100s, Ironman Triathlons, and even longer races.
2. A certain group of runners always wants to stay ahead of the wave. These people run not to be part of any crowd but to set themselves apart from it. As the crowd runs farther, the pacesetters must go farther yet. This leads to the longer and longer races.

The human appetite to run ahead of the pack and to be noticed there is almost insatiable. At the same time, the chances to attract attention in standard racing—100 meters through the marathon—are limited. Few of us were born with or ever develop the speed to succeed there. But almost anyone can run longer.

That's the story of the so-called running boom: more people running longer. Ten years ago, being any kind of distance runner made you unusual enough. Then came the runners-for-exercise, so you advertised your differences from them by racing 10 kilometers. The 10-K races got crowded, so the marathon became the new home for the elite.

Now, as the number of U.S. marathoners climbs toward 100,000, every office and neighborhood has one. Runners looking to stay different have moved on to the ultras. The Western States race has grown so popular that it must limit entries—for a race where the average time is more than 24 hours.

Multi-sport races attract the *avant garde*, too. The Ironman Triathlon in Hawaii—a two-mile ocean swim and 112-mile bike ride leading up to a marathon run—is drawing turnaway crowds as well. And this is not good news to a runner looking for uniqueness.

What next? Revivals of the multi-day runs and the Bunion Derbies? Norris McWhirter, the Guinness man, would admire these runners.

"Americans have such a high level of achievement," he says. Then he adds, "The underachievers are driven into zanier outlets."

The zanier ones are the problem with the Guinness Syndrome. We run in a time of creeping craziness. People who can't run either fast enough or far enough to draw attention to themselves do it with ridiculous variations. We see them racing backwards, or while jumping rope or balancing a bottle of champagne on a tray. We read of them dressing in tuxedoes, gorilla costumes, and bridal gowns. We even hear of nude racers.

No one would deny runners their right to have fun. But some antics go beyond fun and beyond sport, crossing the lines from joy to a joke and from sport to entertainment. These performers ridicule the athletes who run seriously and well.

Pseudo-athletes run for publicity. True athletes run for the challenge and accept publicity as a by-product.

Al Arnold said before climbing Mt. Whitney, "Believe me, I appreciate the publicity. But there are easier ways to attract attention. If I fail, I could be ridiculed. Even if I make it, many will not understand."

Arnold didn't make it, but no runner ridiculed him. We understood that even his failed effort was a noble one. Ridicule is reserved for the exhibitionists.

The main danger in the super-distance phase which running is passing through now is one of attitude. By glorifying these distances too much, we devalue the normal ones and demean runners who can't or won't go beyond them.

The attitude that anyone who runs less than a marathon is less than a complete runner is dangerous. So is the idea that all there is to running is breaking records.

Speaking of award-winning and record-breaking obsessions, sports psychologist Thomas Tutko says, "The emphasis is on the product and not the process. The product is temporary. The trouble with the product is that it always has to be replaced by another. That's a hell of a way to live."

We live in a time, says the author of *The Running Revolution*, when "there no longer are good and bad runners, only fast and slow ones. The real revolution of the 1970s has been the wiping away of slower runners' inferiority complexes. Runners had to become proud of who they were and happy with what they did before they dared put themselves on the line in races."

Perhaps the 1980s should be a time for a second revolution. The first one made it okay not to run too fast—to admire the faster people without feeling intimidated by them. The second revolution should tell us it is okay not to run too far—to admire the super-distance people without needing to imitate them.

ONE IN A MILLION

ROGER BANNISTER, as everyone knows, was the first to break four minutes in the mile. What many people don't remember is who broke it second—and ran faster than Bannister. That was John Landy. The two met after exchanging the record separately.

It was a classic duel of front-runner against follower. Landy led most of the way. Then when he heard accelerating footsteps, he cast a panicked glance to his right—the wrong way. Bannister passed on the other side and won before Landy could recover.

We all make this tactical mistake sometimes. We look the wrong way to see who is beating us instead of seeing that we have already won. We may have long since accepted the fact that we'll never run as fast or as far as the top athletes. But we still look up to them with envy and always feel slow, lazy, and fat by comparison.

The cure: look the other way, back over where you have been.

If you once ran in high school, think of how few old teammates kept running after graduation. The national average probably is fewer than one in 10. Of the survivors who went on to run in college, not more than 10 percent still ran after leaving their teams. This attrition has pushed you into the 99th percentile among runners who started with you. You didn't have to outrun them, only outlast them.

But wait, the numbers get even better. Do you race now—not just enter races but truly *race* them? If so, you're the one current runner in a thousand who does. If you race marathons, you're one in 10,000.

These figures only consider the people who run. Look further to the population as a whole. If you've run for years and you race long distances, you're one in a *million*.

With these odds, you don't need to try anything more spectacular than the modest running you already do. You already have such a big lead that almost no one will ever catch you. You don't need to envy other heroes, because you are one.

V

Victims
of the Road

SEPARATE AND NEVER EQUAL

STATISTICS CLEARLY SHOW women runners to be closing the distance between themselves and men in both numbers and times. But statistics don't reveal one area of inequality which, sadly, may never change. A woman can never run alone in the nicest places (meaning the secluded ones), at dawn or dusk, and feel safe. A man can, a woman can't.

A woman who asks that she not be identified is a running-rights activist. She campaigned for the women's marathon in the Olympics. She serves as a national women's-running official. She writes on women's issues for the magazines. But she still was a woman running alone in a secluded area that morning. She was a target for a predator.

"I had read all the articles about it," she says. "I'd given all the lectures to my own daughters. I'd rehearsed hundreds of times in my own mind what I would do if attacked while out running. And still I wasn't prepared when it happened to me.

"Rounding a blind curve, there he was about 15 yards ahead of me, unbuckling his pants. My first thought was that I had surprised a fellow relieving himself. But an instant later, I realized that was not the case as he turned toward me, exposing himself.

"By that time, my momentum had taken me abreast of him, and I sprinted to get by. He reached out and grabbed at me. I screamed shrilly, and it was as if someone else was screaming. I couldn't believe this was happening. Adrenaline mainlining, I slipped out of his grasp and charged up a hill and into the open . . ."

She ran home and called the police. First they told her that a man fitting this one's description had been threatening women in that area for the last two months—yet women hadn't been warned. Then an officer said, "I hope this incident won't keep you from running along our beautiful bike trail."

And men wonder why women are angry.

This woman says, "I didn't or wouldn't tell anyone to stop running. Don't give up that freedom which men take for granted, but perhaps run with a bit more caution. Don't get complacent, as I believe I did. Stay out in the open if you run alone. Run with a friend at dusk or after dark. Get some Mace, carry it, and use it."

Her last piece of advice: "Report immediately any incident or unusual person you see. But after what happened to me, I wonder: Will it do any good?"

Moving Targets

Few of us comfortably confront our own mortality. Indeed, if we constantly worried about dying, we wouldn't enjoy living. Our need to reassure ourselves about living may explain a quirk of the human mind: We dwell on the trivial so we won't have to think the unthinkable.

While traveling by plane, we fret over delays of minutes, while trusting that the jet is well enough built and guided to stay suspended on a cushion of air.

As we run, we cut corners, jay-run, and ignore lights rather than lose a few seconds. At the same time, we have faith that drivers who share the roads with us are skilled and alert enough not to violate the small space between us and them and mayhem.

Runners worry a lot. We're so busy sorting out our little worries concerning top performance and the things that block it that we have few thoughts left over for the biggest threat facing us. It is not heat or a heart problem—each a fatal but remote possibility—but one that passes within inches of a road runner every few seconds and could kill him with one wrong flick of a steering wheel.

A study by the Insurance Institute for Highway Safety offers chilling statistics on collisions between runners and motor vehicles. It analyzed 60 accidents, involving 65 runners, during a one-year period. Thirty of these runners died of their injuries.

In nearly half of the 60 cases, police said the drivers and runners were equally to blame. Runners appeared to be responsible for 19 accidents, and drivers were at fault 16 times.

According to this report, 15 collisions involved hit-and-run drivers. The persons were charged with driving while drunk or drugged. Six drivers were indicted for vehicular homicide or negligent injury.

More than half of the accidents occurred at night or at dawn or dusk. Runners at least shared the blame for not insuring their visibility.

The most damning evidence, however, was that "more often than not, (victims) were struck while running on roads in the same direction as vehicles."

Moving with traffic is a violation of both the law and common sense. Runners, like all pedestrians, are required to stay on the left side of roads for their own safety.

Dr. Allan F. Williams, the main author of this report, concluded, "Even if ample off-road running opportunities are provided, (runners) will continue to use the road and to (run) at the most convenient hours, including non-daylight hours when the risk of being struck by a vehicle is highest."

Runners will also continue to ignore accident statistics and safety warnings. The Insurance Institute report won't change that, but it should at least remind us again of one survival tactic: Run against traffic. The right side is the *wrong* side for a runner.

Arne's Legacy

IF FITNESS WERE a more exact science, Arne Richards might be running today. The truth is, no one is quite sure what the relationships are among exercise, diet, and heart health. No one has made a final tally of benefits and risks, or drawn up a scientifically sound plan for maximizing the former and minimizing the latter.

So runners stumble through a maze of conflicting advice:

- One expert writes that exercising 30 minutes a week gives "total fitness." Another says good things don't begin to happen until a runner goes at least 30 minutes a *day*.
- A government panel reports that fats in the diet don't hurt most people, while a best-selling author argues for cutting out most fatty foods.
- One doctor calls running a form of "mass suicide," because he has seen a few runners die from it. Other doctors claim that a certain level of training gives absolute protection against fatal heart disease.

To an extent, all of the scientists are offering theories, which is to say, guesswork based on limited evidence. The mistake runners make is reading more certainty into this advice than really exists.

Arne Richards believed too much and ran into the worst kind of trouble. He ran far beyond the amount needed to maintain good health and assumed his heart was protected for life. He, like nearly all runners, also thought there was no such thing as too little fat.

In March 1979, Richards went for a run from which he never returned. He was found dead in a ditch near his Manhattan, Kansas, home.

Runners have died before, but no death ever shocked the survivors more than this one. Arne seemed to have everything going for him: good genes (his parents lived into their 80s), relative youth (he was 46), a low-stress life (he was single and worked as a librarian in a small city), a thin build (he never weighed more than 130 pounds), and a quarter-century of marathon and ultramarathon racing and training (he had raced 50 kilometers within days of his death).

The coroner in Kansas listed the cause of death as "myocardial infarction due to arteriosclerotic cardiovascular disease"—a heart attack caused by narrowing of the arteries.

That finding made the news doubly shocking. Not only had the sport lost one of its pioneers; maybe none of us was safe if he wasn't.

Fortunately, Tom Bassler didn't accept the report of a classic heart attack. Dr. Bassler, a pathologist from Inglewood, California, studied the Richards case at the request of Arne's relatives.

"The autopsy showed a perfectly normal heart," Dr. Bassler said. "In fact, his arteries were thin and pliable like a child's."

So much for the initial guess that Richards' arteries had

clogged. If his heart structure was healthy, what then had killed him?

Bassler blamed Arne's diet: "He was experimenting with a low-fat diet for a month or so. His high mileage and low body fat made that dangerous."

Richards may have developed what the pathologist called "nutritional arrythmia," a metabolic imbalance triggering a disruption of the heartbeat pattern.

"Arne's death fit the pattern of elite-runner's arrythmia," said Bassler. "You get better and better, thinner and thinner, and cut more and more food items out of your diet."

Richards had complained of unusual fatigue shortly before his fatal attack. The doctor said these were "warnings that the body had exhausted its supply of a nutrient (potassium, zinc, or linoleic acid), and a strict diet restriction doesn't allow replacement in time."

Bassler noted that he had reviewed the cases of more than a dozen other marathoners who had developed arrythmias after severely restricting their fat and protein intake. He planned to warn runners away from these extreme diets as a result.

If anything comforting can be said about the Arne Richards tragedy, it is that he continues to be a pioneer even after he is gone. His case may have moved running closer to being an exact science.

COMMITTING RUNNING SUICIDE

YOU HEAR THEM at parties when running enters the conversation.

"So you run," they say. "I used to be a runner myself. Did a 4:22 mile in high school when that was still a class time. It earned me a free ride at State U."

You ask if they run now.

"Naw. I stopped after a year of college. Things got too serious. Running wasn't fun anymore, so I quit for good. None of this marathoning for me. Tennis is my sport now."

You see them at track meets and road races. They walk stiff-legged, sometimes with a slight limp. They stand apart from the runners, watching them intently but feeling left out of their sport. These spectators raced once, but now the racing is gone from their legs. All they can do is stand aside and remember the old races—and dream of recovery for future ones.

These are the subtle victims of running, the ones who committed athletic suicide. No one attacked them. They weren't hit by an errant driver. They had no exotic disease or run of bad luck.

These ex-runners simply and brutally killed their own ambitions and abilities. Some could still run, but can't stand the thought of doing it again; others want desperately to run again, but can't make their legs work.

Chronic psychological and physical injuries arise from the same source: running too far, too fast, too often—until either the mind or the body snaps. But before any snapping occurs, the warning signs are clearly announced.

You alone control your physical and psychological well-being. You can invite damage or prevent it. You decide whether you want to talk at parties about running in the past or present tense. You say whether you watch other racers or race as one of them.

W

Where Next?

FAD OR FOREVER?

As LONGTIME RUNNERS look around them, they see a once-quiet, once-simple sport grown wild. Newer runners see they've stumbled onto a good thing but wonder if it can last. All runners see evidence that running is entering an era of hard times and hard feelings.

Some reasons for concern:

> • Sponsors who poured hundreds of thousands of dollars into running are withdrawing their support, giving us fewer and smaller races.
> • Professional road racing, which began in hopes of making the sport more honest, has bogged down in disputes among athletes and organizers.
> • Businesses formed to cash in on the running boom are going under, making good supplies harder to find.

• Magazines are suing shoe companies, shoe companies are suing each other, and authors are suing publishers. Runners will be the ultimate losers.

• Public officials are discouraging runners from using "their" streets for racing—and sometimes even for training.

• Critics of running are stepping up their attacks as they smell a kill.

For the first time, we hear more talk about what is wrong with running than what's right about it. If this talk only came from outside critics, we wouldn't care, but it bothers us to hear runners talking this way.

We ask, "Where is running headed?" It's usually a worried question, asked out of concern that the sport has taken a wrong turn and is moving toward destruction.

A sign of decline in a sport is when it graduates beyond its internal journals to the front pages of the national press. That means it has become less of a sport and more of a business. Such a sign of trouble appeared when running made headlines in the nation's leading business publication, the *Wall Street Journal*.

Frederick Klein wrote, "The more prosperous a sport becomes, the more likely it is to destroy the reasons for its prosperity."

Running prospered because it was simple and cheap. A runner didn't need any special skills or settings, didn't need a coach or a team to get going. All he needed to start running was a comfortable pair of shoes, open space, and free time.

Running is still running along, but it isn't simple or cheap any more. Its prosperity has taken away some of the attraction that helped it prosper.

WHERE IS RUNNING HEADED? To know where running might be going, we must look back at where it's been.

Twenty years ago, Roger Hamilton felt at home running through the farm country. The farmers may not have understood or cared for his sport, but they appreciated someone who was lean and wiry as they were, and who worked against the elements as they did.

"I felt out of place when I moved to the city," Hamilton says. "There, it was odd to be fit and normal to be fat, odd to move on foot and normal to be moved by wheels. I hid from the drivers by running on tracks and in secluded parks."

Twenty years later, though, the switch is almost total. Every city and suburb has runners who have escaped temporarily from their luxurious prisons. Our numbers have gone up by a factor of 100 since the 1960s. We can run anywhere in any city, anytime, and feel comfortable doing it.

Meanwhile, farm country has taken on some of the worst city traits. Many rural folk move too comfortably from house to vehicle and from vehicle to house. Their health reflects these habits. Fat is in, fit is out.

"I feel odd when I run on my old home ground," says Hamilton, "just as I felt in the 1960s in the city. I go to the emptiest country roads to get away from the stares of people who don't look and act as I do. I have to remind myself that history is on my side. My way has lasted a lot longer than theirs. If I wait long enough, they'll come back around to mine."

Roger saw hopeful signs when he was last in farm country. An adult softball league, started that summer, drew enough men and women to form half a dozen teams. You might not think of softball as heavy exercise, but it's a start.

Hamilton didn't actually see another runner on the streets and roads there. "But I did see fresh footprints besides my own on my favorite dirt road." If one person makes a break from the prison of physical complacency, others are sure to follow in rural areas as they did earlier in the cities and suburbs. New runners won't join a fad when they start. They'll leave a fad behind.

When someone tries to tell you that running is a fad that will soon go the way of the Hoola Hoop and the Twist, you first laugh. Then you say you've been hearing that for years, and during that time the running population has multiplied.

Next you say that running has three strong forces keeping it going and growing:

1. *It is addictive.* A runner becomes what poet Emily Dickinson called "an inebriate of air." Once you have learned to drink it in eight times the amounts you take while sitting down, and you feel the cleansing effects this has on you in every way, you're hooked. Few current runners will ever quit.

2. *It is contagious.* Everyone who runs is a carrier. One person sees another run and says, "If he can do it, so can I." If every addicted runner infects two people, think how many runners there will be by the year 2000.

3. *It is hereditary.* Amby Burfoot, a Boston Marathon winner, says his son's first words were, "Mommy run." At two, he already thought it normal and natural for his parents to run every day instead of lighting cigarettes or growing fat. Our generation has had to change bad habits. The next one has a running start on good ones simply by imitating parents.

Finally, when someone tells you fitness is a fad, quote Dr. Peter Wood. He works with the Stanford Heart Disease Prevention Program and has run for 40 of his 50 years.

Dr. Wood writes in his book *Run to Health*, "If we look at man, we see an animal with powerful legs, clearly designed to run. We see an animal that has effectively used those legs over the centuries, over the evolutionary ages—until some 60 years ago when everyone climbed aboard the automobile and running became rather quaint except for a few young athletes.

"From then on, it was all downhill as cars filled the roads, the populace gradually put on weight, and coronary heart disease became first a significant medical problem and finally the greatest health menace of modern times."

Dr. Wood's view: "The 'craze' has been one of *inactivity*, making the running revolution an overdue return to biological sanity."

Kenny Moore noticed a return to another kind of sanity before other writers did. He wrote in *Sports Illustrated* several years ago of runners rejecting the crowds and hype of the sport's craze phase.

"There are runners now, usually those who have run for years, who no longer come to big races, who feel them to be perverted simply by the crush, the leveling of numbers," Moore said. He predicted that "we may see the stream dividing, one small branch slipping off into the forest."

Time has proven him wrong in only one respect: *Many* streams have branched off. As a growing number of runners return to a quieter approach, these various branches may now hold more people than the old mainstream did.

The new breed of runner has decided to think small and simple, to be his own boss and hero, to take only what he absolutely needs from the marketplace of running and to veto the rest, to look critically at anyone who tries to tell him something or sell him something.

Ed Fox, publisher of *Track and Field News*, disagrees with the earlier statement that "running isn't simple or cheap any more." He says that is only true with one branch of running. "For the person who runs because of the physical and emotional pleasures and benefits derived, and feels no need to test his machismo or see how he compares against others in his age bracket, sex division or whatever, it's still cheap—especially if you feel no need to indulge in running fashions."

Fox's point is that most of the new expense and complications are optional. A runner can buy or do almost anything, but still *needs* very little.

The runner whose needs are simple and few is here to stay. He isn't going to let running die, but he's going to make it change. He isn't going to bend to the wishes of businessmen or promoters. They'll have to bend to serve him as his numbers grow.

WHERE ARE YOU GOING?

NOTICE THAT ALL of the trouble signs listed earlier centered on the business and promotion of running. This is a shakedown period in these areas. Some people who rushed in to capitalize on the sport's popularity are being shaken out as the boom quiets. But we runners needn't worry too much about that.

Where is running headed? The best answer is another question: "Where is *your* running going?" That's what matters. None of us has to suffer the whole sport's growing pains. You only have to deal with your own. If you have two good legs and a place and a time to use them, you don't need much more.

Jim Fixx has earned a fortune by writing about running. But he was a runner first, and his sympathies remain those of a runner and not a tycoon.

In a *Runner* magazine interview, Fixx said, "I haven't been thinking about improving my performances for some time. I've sort of come to look at this activity as my running rather than my training. That must mean something, but I don't know what."

After a pause, Fixx guessed at what it meant to runners in general: "We're now metabolizing running into our lives, like brushing our teeth. Fewer people may race in the future, and certainly there'll be less cocktail-party conversation about running."

This is the direction of running's growth—toward, in Fixx's view, "becoming a routine part of American life." It is quieting down and settling in to stay. The runners who remain will be the quiet and settled ones.

X

X-Ray Vision

MARK TWAIN LIVED AND WROTE long before pop-psychology terms came into everyday language. Yet he gave as good an example of neurosis as anyone has since.

Twain said a cat that sits on a hot stove will never do it again. That's smart. But the cat will never sit on a *cold* stove, either, and that isn't so smart.

A once-burned runner gets neurotic if he won't go back to the scene of a failure and take a chance that the danger has cooled down. A smart one goes back there and builds successes from old failures.

Ron Clarke, the Australian who once held more than a dozen world records, called success and failure "the twin imposters." He said success isn't as good as it seems if it limits us. Failure isn't as bad when it teaches.

Failure is painful. However, it drives us to find other, better paths leading away from the pain. Any runner who survives a few years of running has known failure and has taken alternate routes to escape it. But he never forgets where he's once gone wrong or quits worrying about making the same detours again.

Old phobias linger. These psychological scars are as real and permanent as the marks left on a leg after catching another runner's spikes. You can't make any of these scars go away. But you can shrink them to more attractive size by talking them out.

We fear most the things we don't understand—the unknown, invisible, the dark, and the sinister. The enemy isn't nearly so fearsome when it comes out of the shadows and stands in the daylight.

Phobia: "I'm getting fat. Rolls of lard tumble over my belt and jiggle grossly around my upper legs."

Fact: By any standard considered normal, you probably are not now overweight. You may appear heavy by the unreal standards of bigtime long-distance running, but these people were born skinny. You could go on an 800-calorie-a-day diet and never look like them. Why try? Runners should be sensitive to weight, since each pound does make a difference. But if you take care of your running, the pounds will take care of themselves. If you're running well, you can't be too fat.

Phobia: "I'll peak out. And without steady improvement, I'll lose interest. I'll see that I've done everything, been everywhere, and that nothing in the future could match the past."

Fact: Only after you quit banging your head against your ceiling do you start to understand what running really is. You can't see that until you take your eyes off the watch and notice where you are going.

The more you see, the more there is to be seen. The more you learn, the more there is to be learned. The more you do, the more there is behind you. So you can always go back over old trails and see things along them that you missed the first time—or the first hundred times—you passed that way.

PHOBIA: "I fear that I'm always doing too little, too slowly— that minutes and seconds are slipping away from me as I get older."

Fact: Minutes and seconds don't count for much when measured against a running career lasting years. A few minutes here or there don't matter. What matters is the way they add up. In a year's time, less than an hour of running a day adds up to more than two weeks on your feet. That does count.

What counts in racing is effort. Times inevitably slow down as you age, but effort remains constant. If you race as well as you can with the resources you have available at the moment, you've done as well as you ever could, no matter what the watch might show.

PHOBIA: "I'll have the Final Injury, the big one that makes me a bitter cripple who stands beside the road and envies those who can still run."

Fact: You could get hit by an early-morning garbage truck, a newspaper-delivery van or a bleary-eyed commuter. But those things don't count. They are accidents, and accidents are very rare in this sport. Look only at what might happen as a direct result of running. You've had almost every injury known to sports medicine, from broken toe to chondromalacia to sciatica. Many of them have knocked you down, but none of them has knocked you out. Very few problems in this game are permanent. And none need to be if you listen to what your body tells you—be aware of the warnings.

PHOBIA: "I'll look bad. I'll make a fool of myself. People will laugh at me."

Fact: What's the worst that could happen? You might grow old and quirky in your running, and newer and more hip athletes might dismiss you as 20 years out of date. That shouldn't bother you. Remember that when you started, lots of people thought of you as a young fool, never guessing that your vision then was 20 years ahead of its time.

LASTING IMPRESSIONS

THE GREATEST VALUES OF RUNNING have little to do with the physical act. They result from the time spent at it, the way the runner takes the run and is moved by it. The lessons of the long-distance runner could translate easily to other activities which give:

- A chance to be alone.
- A need to be patient.
- A way to be simple.
- A time to be humble.
- A place to be heroic.

ALONE. "Loneliness of the long-distance runner" is the cliché we present to the world. People may think loneliness is something—like blisters and dehydration and stiff calf muscles—that we have to tolerate to be runners.

We do spend lots of time by ourselves. But no one should feel sorry for us. We aren't lonely. More likely, we feel lonely only when we're lost in a faceless crowd. We go out alone by choice.

Lonely and alone aren't the same. We look at them as opposites, the first negative and the second positive. Most of us feel lonely only as we wander through crowds that don't know our names and don't care to learn them. The crowd decides where we'll go, and what we'll see and hear there. It thinks for us.

We don't get many chances to be alone, to take charge of

our own thoughts and actions. We don't get to decide where we'll go—when and how, and what we'll do there—without following a program someone else sets. We get little chance to clear our paths and our heads of the clutter from a crowded, noisy world.

Running gives those chances. Every day, you get to run away by yourself. You leave behind the crowd and its orders. You put distance between yourself and the newspapers, magazines, and books that bring you other people's thoughts. You escape the radio and TV, with their packaged voices. You get away from the phone, which can invade your day at any other time.

For an hour a day, you take full command of and responsibility for what you do and think. It is your quietest and calmest and most productive hour. That's when you make friends with yourself and prepare to go back into the crowd on more peaceful terms.

Everyone doesn't need to run. But everyone owes himself that one hour in every 24 to be alone.

PATIENT. You can't have whatever you want, whenever you want it. Scarcity, not abundance, is the law of this world.

Runners have always known what others are just finding out—that energy is scarce. We runners are always on the edge of our own energy crisis. Our fuel doesn't flow from a gas pump. We have to produce it ourselves, and the supply is so short that we're on permanent rationing.

We save fuel by obeying speed limits. We call this limit "pace." Each of us has a most efficient pace that's neither too fast nor too slow. We burn too much fuel either by straining against the top speed limit or holding back against the bottom one. We use fuel best at a pace that feels gentle, comfortable, right.

No watch or schedule can say just what that pace should be. The only way to know it is to feel it. No two runners have the same limit, and no one runner has the same limit from day to day, or even from minute to minute within a run.

The second way we runners save energy is by spreading out our efforts. We may total two full weeks of running a year, but we don't think in these rather impressive and frightening terms. What we think about are the little pieces that build this total: 30 to 60 mintues of running a day. Anyone could do that much. The trick is doing it today and tomorrow and the next day and . . .

The patient person sees past, present, and future all at once. He knows that lots of little, unhurried steps add up to big leaps.

SIMPLE. So much of life is now defined by what we have: job, house, address, degrees, titles, clothes, cars. None of that counts when we run. We're stripped down to what we are, which is a body and a mind facing the raw elements of time, distance, and environment.

The pleasures we get from a run are both free and priceless. We can have them any day, but no amount of money can buy them. Only effort can.

The road and the runner's body are like a painter's canvas and brush, a writer's paper and pen, or a sculptor's granite and chisel. They are common raw materials—nothing until the artist makes something of them. Anyone can pick up the materials, but it takes special care to turn them into art.

One definition of art is simply an uncommon thing made from common materials. An artist is one who brings order and beauty to the random, chaotic events of his life, and who sees common things in uncommon ways.

By these definitions, the runner is an artist. He makes his pleasure from the simplest of acts. He makes the best piece of art from what he has available at the moment. This has nothing to do with the new Porsche or the battered 1963 Volkswagen he might own, or whether he wears an M.D. after his name or has his name on food stamps.

Myles & Kathleen
Winnie & Paddy Jordan

Pat & Mary D...mp

May Evans

Colt & Zann
Myt & Annay
Paul & Knight
Pete Zig
Jenny & Mary
Peter & Kelbert
John & ...
John & Ann ...
Pho & Bredar
Jack & Patricia
Frank = Kay
Ann — Doyle Cullam
Mapella Doran & Dann
Frank & Eileen Downey

No one can buy artistic talent, but anyone can produce art.

HUMBLE. No matter how many steps a runner has behind him, he's never more than one away from his last. Everyone needs a breakdown once in a while to show him he doesn't have everything figured out.

You never have every mystery solved—not everyone else's, not even your own. You learn that lesson in every bad run and every failed race. This sport always can find ways to humble you just when you think you have all the answers.

You're always, as George Sheehan says, "peeling the onion." Stripping away one layer of mystery just uncovers a new one. You don't have enough running and racing in you to get down to the core. Even if you did, you would have forgotten the top lessons by the time you got to the bottom ones.

This is as it should be. Knowing how small we are helps us grow. We need to make peace with the flawed persons we are instead of fighting to be perfect.

HEROIC. Running has no shortage of winners. Winning isn't reserved for the person who finishes first overall or for those who come in first in their divisions. Everyone who runs can feel like a winner.

This doesn't mean that everyone automatically wins. If they did, their "victories" wouldn't mean anything. This sport, like all sports, carries risks of losing. But this one, unlike most others, gives everyone an equal chance to win. That's because its standards are both objective and personal. Runners don't have to measure themselves against other people, but only against distance and time. They don't have to beat anyone else to win, but only to better their own records.

"I have found my hero, and I am him," is almost a cliché in running now. But it's still a rare idea in sports as a whole. Many people still have heroes instead of being one. Many rank themselves, or let themselves be ranked, against everyone else doing what they do. Some let themselves think in terms of what they can't do and not what they can. Some never let themselves be proud of themselves.

Everyone needs something he does himself which makes him proud, even if it is only to run a mile farther or a minute faster than before. He needs something no one else can do for him.

Lots of people can run faster than you do. But no one can run for you, no one can run exactly as you do, no one can beat you except yourself, no one can break your personal records, and no one can fully share your happiness and pride in running done well.

Y

Yours for Years

The Endless Run

Ron Hill has shown how fast he can run. The British marathoner once ran a time that still ranks among the world's best, even though he recorded it in 1970. His course record at Boston stood for five years. He competed in three Olympic Games.

All of this speed-record setting is behind him now. Hill is well past 40 years old and is a dozen minutes over the times of his prime. He never held a world marathon mark or won an Olympic title, so his name only makes the footnotes in the history of the event.

However, Hill runs on. He continues to add to his most impressive record each day he runs. This one is measured not by speed but by persistence, not by minutes and seconds but by years.

Hill hasn't missed a day's run since 1964. His streak of consecutive running days totals more than 6000. He has run twice on most of those days and has totaled 100 miles or more most weeks.

Think about those numbers: His streak began before most current high-school runners were born. Hill quit taking days off in his mid-20s, stayed perfect throughout his 30s and continues that way in his 40s. He has run daily through four Olympiads.

This type of record earns little positive attention for Hill and others like him who value his kind of consistency. *Sports Illustrated* once turned over a dozen of its expensive pages to an examination of "running addicts." William Oscar Johnson made them sound neurotic.

Chet Vorspan, a psychiatric social worker, followed with an article on "The Obsessive-Compulsive Runner" in the *Minnesota Distance Runner*. Vorspan, who admits to having "O-C" symptoms himself, wrote, "As more and more people with obsessive-compulsive personality traits get into running, their compulsiveness is being transferred to their running. Instead of being a healthy outlet, their running becomes another daily ritual which begins to exert more and more control over the runner."

Vorspan pointed to streak-keepers as examples: "The O-C runner finds it increasingly difficult to take a day off from running. Streaks achieve a life of their own, until the O-C runner actually loses the ability to terminate a streak voluntarily. I have known runners who would not or could not let a serious injury prevent them from taking their daily run, resulting in a gradual worsening of the injury."

No one is more righteous than a reformed addict. Derek Clayton overcame his own obsessive-compulsive tendencies (including 200-mile training weeks before his record marathons of the 1960s) and now views other addicts with disdain.

"I know one bloke," Clayton said at a running clinic, "who won't even let himself have a day off. He runs right through everything—illness, injury, fatigue. This is bloody crazy. How can anyone have fun in this game if he's that obsessed with it?"

Clayton, Vorspan, and Johnson imply that running every day is a disease. It can be carried to that extreme, of course. But there is little evidence that Ron Hill is afflicted. As a high-performance athlete, he knows better than to force himself through serious injury or illness. That would hurt his performances, and the record shows they haven't suffered. The most significant feature of Hill's streak may be that he has gone since 1964 without *needing* days off.

Hill has no visible abnormality in his character that has driven him to run more than 6000 days in a row. He simply has made his run a normal, natural, healthy part of each day. Wanting to run daily is no more "sick" than wanting to eat breakfast and take a shower. Being able to run that often is the problem, and Hill has solved it for years.

CHASING GHOSTS

TONY OAKES DOESN'T JUST BELIEVE in ghosts. He knows they exist. He sees them often, and even when he can't see them he feels them in the places where they live.

"I don't mean to be morbid," he says, "because I don't feel that way at all when I visit my ghosts. They give me a warm, happy feeling of knowing that no one and nothing he does passes away unless he or it is forgotten."

We leave something of ourselves behind wherever we go. The traces aren't monuments to ourselves that others can see—like the buildings of an architect or the books of a writer, or even the food wrappers of a hiker on a trail or the spray-painted graffiti of a city kid in a subway. These have no more life than the tombstones in a cemetery. The true remains are the living, moving, breathing, laughing, crying, playing, eating, sleeping presences that only we can see, living every place we've ever been.

"As a kid," Oakes says, "I imagined a movie was being made of my life. Part of the time, I was its star. The rest of the time, I was its director or cameraman. I acted as if everything I did was going on permanent record. I now know that such a movie really was made. I turn it on almost every day.

"Its best reels are the old ones—the classics from times when I was young and everything was new."

Tony Oakes climbs the fence into the stadium and lets the years wait for him outside. Suddenly there has been no Kennedy or King killings, no Vietnam, no Watergate. It is 1961 again, and he is 17 years old.

"I know I can't live in the past," he says, "but for a little while, I can visit it. I can pretend it is still there, and so am I."

He chooses to think it is May 20th, 1961, again. It came, as one day tagging along behind another, and only after it was gone did he see what it meant.

Tony was then and still is a runner. If he's lucky, a runner is given a few days out of thousands in his career when everything goes perfectly, when he combines conditioning and opportunity and luck in just the right way. Then he performs better than he ever had before and ever will again.

"I had one of my days on May 20th, 1961," says Oakes. "Everything I did before as a runner got me ready for that day, and everything I've done since has been touched by it."

He won a state high-school mile championship that day in record time, before a large crowd. No one is here to watch him run again in the same stadium all these years later. If anyone had been, he would have seen what looked like just another middle-aged jogger doing ritual laps on the track. Tony knows better. He is rerunning his old movie.

A bouncy all-weather surface now covers the red crushed-brick track he had used, and metric markings have made his old event, the mile, obsolete. But the stadium's outlines are the same as before. The infield sits six feet lower than the track, which puts runners above the heads of the infield crowd. Oakes feels heroic here, even as he runs easily and alone.

Concrete grandstands circle three-fourths of the track, and a black scoreboard towers above the north turn. Years later, Tony can still see his name spelled out in lights here.

The stadium may look empty. But he fills it with his own pictures and sounds from 1961, memories preserved better than any videotape or stereo recording could hold them.

Events, like people, only die when no one remembers them anymore. A part of Tony Oakes would die if he forgot his run here on that May 20th. That's why he comes back to visit. He has to carry out this ritual of touching old ground and seeing the friendly ghosts who live here. He links past and present by mixing old sweat with new.

Oakes runs through the neighborhood where he lived in 1963. Time has beaten Fay Way down a little more, and the faces of the people living here are darker now than they were then. But the house at 355 has resisted the general decline around it. It has a new coat of paint, white in place of its old red. The greasy auto parts are gone from the driveway, though traces of the old grease remain. It now is a family home, not the runners' commune it had been.

"There were as many as eight of us living at 355 Fay Way that summer," Oakes recalls. "I slept in the garage with the owner of the place. I took the garage because I couldn't afford more than $35 a month rent. He stayed there because he could make more money renting out an inside bedroom instead of sleeping in it.

"I see a film of my old self there in that garage—a 20-year-old boy with a skin-tight haircut, legs as yet untouched by injury and a face unlined by real-life worries. My biggest worry was that I might not get a PR in the next race."

Two blocks from the house is La Loma Park—really little

more than a baseball field with extra grass in the outfield. Tony did 95 percent of his running there in 1963, circling the park three times every mile. He went as far as 10 miles a day around the rows of newly planted trees which marked his course, and never saw another runner besides his friends from Fay Way.

Oakes tells of "a girl of unknown name and background— I choose to remember her as Rosa from the Philippines— who came there several days a week to watch her little brother play. Rosa was 11 or 12 then, and she asked me about my running and even ran a few laps herself. I remember her because so few people did that in 1963—either ran or asked about it. That little girl must be about 30 years old now, with children of her own as old as her brother had been then."

Tony had plotted a course which stayed to the outside of the seedling trees. Those trees have grown enough to shade the old circuit which seems much smaller than it had then. He circles the park a few times, chasing the ghost of a 20-year-old boy who once ran there in bare feet.

Then Oakes runs quickly back to now, happy to have seen his old self for a little while, but much happier to be where he has come and who he has become in the years since 1963.

Z

Zest for Life

The Run Has Just Begun

SOME OF THE best running ground in the world lies on the thumb of land which sticks out into the Pacific near Monterey, California. The 17-Mile Drive follows the rugged coastline and attracts almost as many runners as motor-driven tourists. Even better are the miles of empty trails in Del Monte Forest.

Decades ago, the Del Monte Corporation hacked these trails from the dense pine and oak forest. This first clearing of trees and brush was hard work. Once done, though, all it took to keep the paths in shape was a quick scraping to clear away fallen limbs and smooth over erosion.

There may be a lesson here for runners. We blaze a new trail by getting into shape for the first time. The first pass through virgin territory is hard and often painful work. That doesn't mean, however, that all running must always hurt.

183

In fact, in the interest of long-term running, most of it must involve only modest but regular effort.

In repeated trips over old ground, the emphasis shifts from plowing to grooming. We run not to hack out new pathways but to maintain and improve existing ones. We run mainly to brush away obstacles, the main ones being injury and loss of interest from working too hard, too often. If we stay healthy and eager, we keep running. If we keep the path beneath us free of debris, the future takes care of itself.

MOVING BODIES

THE LAWS OF INERTIA apply to the whole natural world. Any body at rest wants to stay at rest, and any body in motion wants to keep moving. This goes for running bodies as all others.

· Ron Clarke, the busiest world-record-setter of modern times, once said that the only hard thing about running was taking the first step out the door. Making this break from resting inertia is the barrier that stops most people from ever becoming runners, and it even causes longtime runners to hesitate every morning before breaking into motion. We start more from habit and memory than from desire.

While the first step may be the hardest, the next ones aren't much easier. The body so recently at rest fights the motion. It loses its kinks reluctantly. Only after two or three miles are we ready to run as we're meant to move—smoothly and powerfully. It takes us that long to warm up. Only then do we get that wonderful feeling that this body in motion can stay in motion forever.

It can't do that, of course. The body gradually tires as it approaches its limits of motion. The moving body wants to keep going, and it fights the need to stop. This is when the mind must restrain the runaway body, like a jockey riding a temperamental racehorse.

Just as the rider must go to the whip to get the horse out of the gate, he must later rein in its excitement to avoid destruction. Smart running involves knowing how to start and knowing when to stop—to save the ability and interest to run again another day.

This running pattern of halting start, flowing middle, and reluctant stop repeats itself day after day. It's basic to running, both daily and career-wise.

Careers run this way:

* *The decision.* "Do I start? It looks kind of nice to be out there moving freely. I know I should get some exercise. But I'm so busy, where do I find the time?" For every 100 people who think they might or should run, one does. Inertia keeps the other 99 resting bodies at rest.
* *The first steps.* "There, I'm running. But I don't feel so hot. My legs ache. My lungs burn. I'm clumsy. I thought this stuff was supposed to be fun." The early part isn't fun for anyone. After being hauled around most of the time, we have to learn to carry ourselves again. That takes a month for every year we have spent riding.
* *The easy part.* "Hey, I'm in shape! I can glide through distances that once were impossible. I can hold a pace for 10 miles that I wasn't able to run for one before. This running is great!" This is the euphoric stage, the time when runners can't stop talking about this miracle they've discovered.
* *The critical part.* "What's happening to me? I was doing so well, then I upped my mileage, added some interval work, and now I'm falling apart. My times have quit improving. I can't go on like this, but I can't imagine stopping." This is when a runner must come to terms with the realities of running.

No one passes through this critical stage unchanged. Some runners quit in depression or disgust, never to return. The wiser ones adjust their theories and practices, and come away from the crisis eager to move on.

The first group thinks that a Golden Age has passed.

Rollin Workman, a runner from Ohio, says, "The memory of a supposed Golden Age is usually a memory of one's youth, when everything was new and exciting and seemingly filled with possibilities which were felt to be unlimited. When people realize that the alternatives are limited, the memory of a lost Golden Age begins to appear."

Such a runner may mourn the loss of his Golden Age, but others survive to see that the best running is yet to come. If you've survived, you now know that the true Golden Age of running wasn't a single block of time that came once, stayed for a couple of years, and went away forever. This Golden Age lies on the other side of the mountain—beyond the hardest work and longest distances and fastest times, when you settle down to enjoy the smaller and better things the sport offers.

WINNERS NEVER QUIT

No ATHLETE QUITS while he is winning. So the way to keep all athletes from quitting is to make us all winners. This requires broader definitions of winning and losing than the athletic world generally uses.

Consider these redefinitions:

> • Winning is *realizing you have already won* something by being in the race. You may not finish ahead of many others, but you have already beaten a much bigger pack of people who choose to move on wheels instead of by their own power.
>
> Losing is not starting, but being content to talk about what might be or what might have been . . . if.

• Winning is *finishing the distance* you set for yourself, however humble it might be. Speed is a gift, but endurance and persistence are learned. Finishing is a victory of strong spirit over weak flesh.

Losing is dropping out for no other reason than a weak will. Giving in to moderate inconvenience or mild discomfort is defeat.

• Winning is *measuring yourself against yourself.* It is, first, learning to take pride in your improvements, no matter how small. Later it is taking pleasure in more subtle measures of victory which have little to do with time and place.

Losing is matching yourself against everyone else who runs. This is self-defeating, because few people ever win this way—and those who do don't stay on top very long.

• Winning is counting the number of athletes ahead of you and *recognizing your relative ability.* You look up to them for advice and inspiration, without viewing them with feelings of envy or inferiority.

Losing is being intimidated out of the sport by those ahead of you or counting as inferior anyone who comes in later.

• Winning is *working with other athletes* so all of your results are better than any of you could have gotten alone. It is in one sense selfish; you use someone to raise yourself. But it is constructive competition in the sense that it can lift everyone.

Losing is cutting someone else down so you can look taller. It is interfering in any way, physically or psychologically, with another's progress.

• Winning is *accepting the results* as they come, knowing that an occasional bad run will come even to those who look at running as "fun." These bad runs are important as contrasts to help you appreciate the good ones.

Losing is choosing to ignore the real results and to quote exaggerated ones instead.

• Winning is *learning from your bad experiences.* They often teach better than the good ones, because they force you to look for relief.

Losing is refusing to accept failure as a teacher to examine the reasons for failing.

• Winning is *standing on the shoulders of the giants.* It is absorbing the written and spoken lessons of people who have run before, instead of using up an entire career resolving by trial and error the puzzles that already have been solved.

Losing is refusing to share with others your solutions to training and racing puzzles.

• Winning is *continuing to stay fit* after fate has decided that you are past your prime and will never again break a personal record. It is going on when there are no races left to run.

Losing is setting goals you either can't reach or can touch too easily. Goals are stopping places if they're made too rigid and important. If you don't reach them, you stop from frustration; if you reach them too quickly, you stop with no other peaks left to climb.

• Winning is *knowing you are only as good as your last run.* The good effects and feelings don't store well, so you have to renew them all the time. Mediocre fresh efforts are far better than spectacular stale ones.

Losing is living in the past. It is trying to restore old glories to the condition they were in during their short life.

Winning is surviving, and in the long haul, a survivor is the best anyone can be. Youth fades, speed declines, medals tarnish. What survives is the act of running itself.

Index